Programmer's Guide to LISP

Other TAB books by the author:

- No. 771 *Integrated Circuits Guidebook*
- No. 861 *Display Electronics*
- No. 960 *IC Function Locator*
- No. 1000 *57 Practical Programs & Games in BASIC*
- No. 1050 *The Most Popular Subroutines in BASIC*
- No. 1055 *The BASIC Cookbook*
- No. 1085 *24 Tested, Ready-to-Run Game Programs in BASIC*
- No. 1095 *Programs in BASIC for Electronic Engineers, Technicians & Experimenters*
- No. 1099 *How To Build Your Own Working 16-Bit Microcomputer*

DEDICATION

I would like to thank my friends who somehow understood me when I was either wiriting or deep into computer printouts. I would especially like to thank Alec, who coauthors other computer language texts with me.

Programmer's Guide to LISP
by Ken Tracton

TAB BOOKS Inc.
BLUE RIDGE SUMMIT, PA. 17214

FIRST EDITION

FIRST PRINTING—AUGUST 1980

Copyright © 1980 by TAB BOOKS Inc.

Printed in the United States of America

Reproduction or publication of the content in any manner, without express permission of the publisher, is prohibited. No liability is assumed with respect to the use of the information herein.

Library of Congress Cataloging in Publication Data

Tracton, Ken.
    Programmer's guide to LISP.

    Includes index.
    1. LISP (Computer program language) I. Title.
QA76.73.L23T7   001.6'424   79-17237
ISBN 0-8306-9761-6
ISBN 0-8306-1045-6 pbk.

Preface

If you have access to a computer with the LISP language, you can start to use LISP as you read this book. The best way to learn any language is to start using it right away.

The first section of this book has a question and answer format. There are also reviews and plenty of examples in this section. The second section covers many diverse programs and routines in LISP.

The reader who sincerely wants to learn and goes through every question and answer will have all the information needed to understand any LISP program.

Near the end of the question and answer sections I state that different LISP systems might handle some things in a slightly different fashion. For example, when reviewing the programs don't be surprised to see in certain places the " ' " symbols. This has exactly the same meaning as the word quote as described in this text. The LISP interpreter used while preparing this book used this symbol instead of the more common quote function. All programs and definitions have been tested on a CDC-CYBER Computer.

Ken Tracton

Contents

Part One: LISP 9

Algebraic Functions 10
Expressions 13
Atoms 16
Symbols 18
Lists 21
Sublists 25
Recursion 27
The LISP System 29
Subexpressions 32
First Review 34
Functions in LISP 35
Common LISP Functions 39
Logic 61
LISP Parameters 63
List Processing 65
Predicates 71
Second Review 74
How Predicates Are Used 76
Recursive Functions 78
Recursive List Processing 81
Logic: Section Two 83
Dot Notation 86
The General List 87
Two List Recursion 89
Type Functions 89
More Review 92
Programming 93
More on Programming 95
Input/Output 106
And More Review 108
More LISP 112
Artificial Intelligence 115

Part Two: Programs and Examples 121

Add 122
Annular Moment of Inertia 124
Annular Polar Moment 126
Atom Check 128
Atom Member of a List 130
Circular Polar Moment 132
Complex Addition 134
Complex Conjugate 136
Complex Division 138
Complex Multiplication 140
Complex Reciprocal 142
Complex Subtraction 144
Complex Square 146
Complex Square Root 148
COSH(X) 150
COTH(X) 152
Count 154
CSCH(X) 156
Depth of Parentheses 158
Derivative of ACOS(X) 159
Derivative of ACOT(X) 161
Derivative of ASECH(X) 162
Derivative of ATAN(X) 164
Derivative of ATANH (X) 166
Display the Nth Atom 168
Factorial 170
Falling Object 171
Fetch 173
Inductance 175
Imaginary Part of a Complex Number 176
Insertion of an Atom No. 1 178
Insertion of an Atom No. 2 179
Joule's Law 180
List of First Atoms 182
Mapping (One to One) 183
Matching 184
Vector Value 185
Parallel Resistance 186
Percentage Change 187
Power (Any Positive Integer) 188
Power (Primitive) 190
Psychiatrist 191
Real Part of a Complex Number 193
Real to Complex Conversion 194
Rectangular Polar Moment 196
Remove 197
Remove an Atom From a List 198
Remove the Numbers 199
Replacement 200
Reverse 201
SECH(X) 202
SINH(X) 203

   TANH(X) 204
   Vector Addition 205
   Vector Cross Product 206
   Vector Multiplied by a Scalar 208
   Vector Test for all Zeros 209

Index 210

Part One: LISP

The LISP language, probably the best-know artificial intelligence language, was invented by John McCarthy. LISP is generally considered to be a process-description language. It is used in artificial intelligence because it is precise, unambiguous and relatively easy to learn. The whole concept of artificial intelligence would be lost if it were not for LISP and the other LISP-like languages.

Statements in LISP (with the exception of what is called the 0-level) are always enclosed in parentheses. Such an enclosure is termed a list and the items contained are called elements of the list. The LISP language is a prefix language where functions preceed their arguments. This is somewhat similar to the RPN notation in calculators but in reverse.

Of the many functions available in LISP, most of them are mnemonics. Care should be taken in learning them in order to avoid confusion. The elements in LISP are generally called ATOMS and lists and ATOMS are termed S-expressions (symbolic-expressions).

There are mathematical functions that use words instead of symbols. Some functions construct lists while other functions take lists apart. There are ways to inhibit function evaluation and ways of causing function evaluation. Execution of the function is termed evaluation. There are also special functions called predicates which are like predicates in languages. These functions are either true or false. Usually the word false is replaced with the word NIL.

ALGEBRAIC FUNCTIONS

Is the logarithm of X written in BASIC as LOG(X)?
Yes, all functions in BASIC are written as "function" name then in parentheses the argument of the function so named (Fig. 1).

Fig. 1. FUNCTION NAME (X)

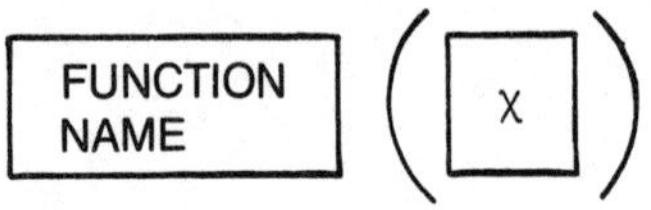

Is the logarithm of X written in LISP as LOG(X)?
No, all functions in LISP are written as ("function name" "variable") (Fig. 2). Therefore the logarithm of X is written as:
(LOG X)

Fig. 2. (FUNCTION NAME X)

Does this apply to all mathematical functions in LISP?
Yes, all functions are enclosed in parentheses.
How is the sum of X and Y written in LISP (Fig. 3)?
(PLUS X Y)

Fig. 3. (PLUS X Y)

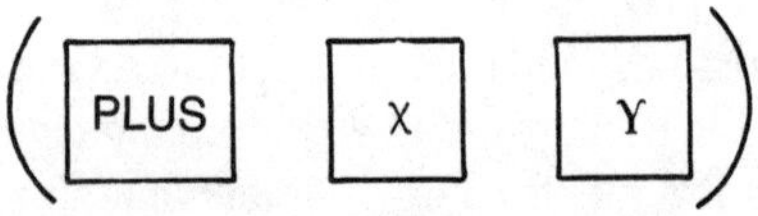

In regards to algebraic manipulation how is LISP different from BASIC?
BASIC, FORTRAN and APL use an algebraic language. The common functions such as sum, difference, quotient and product are handled in a special way in order to increase the speed in which the program can be written. In these algebraic languages, primitive algebraic functions are written without parentheses. LISP, however, is a "functional" language. All functions, primitive or not, are written with parentheses.

How do you write the log of sine of X in LISP?
Write with the parentheses (Fig. 4):
(LOG(SIN X))

Fig. 4.

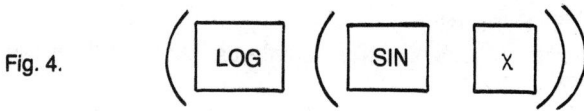

How would you write X/Z-Y in LISP?
Write this expression as:
(QUOTIENT X (DIFFERENCE Z Y))
How would you write X-Y *Z in LISP?
You would write (Fig. 5):
(DIFFERENCE X (TIMES Y Z))

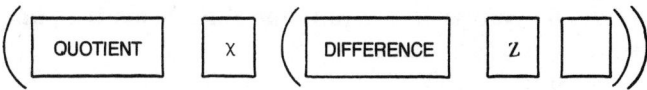

Fig. 5.

Can any arithmetic expression be written in LISP in this way?

Yes, any function that is arithmetic in nature, including parenthesized expressions, can be written in this fashion.

How would you write (A-B) * (Z-X)?
Write this expression as (Fig. 6):
(TIMES(DIFFERENCE A B) (DIFFERENCE Z X))

([TIMES] ([DIFFERENCE] [A] [B]) ([DIFFERENCE] [Z] [X]))

Fig. 6.

Can you write A *(-B) in LISP?
Yes, write A * (-B) as (Fig. 7):
(TIMES A (MINUS B))

Fig. 7. ([TIMES] [A] ([MINUS] [B]))

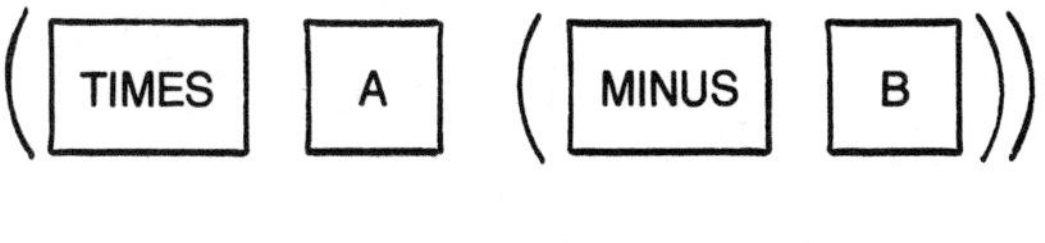

What is the difference between "DIFFERENCE" and "MINUS"?

The DIFFERENCE function is the same as ordinary subtraction, while the "unary minus" function is written as (Fig. 8):

11

(MINUS "variable")
Therefore, to denote a negative number in LISP write:
(MINUS X)
And never (-X)

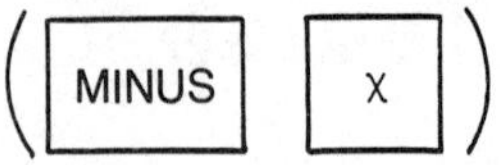

$$(\boxed{\text{MINUS}}\ \boxed{X})$$

Fig. 8.

Do the algebraic functions in LISP always have two arguments?

Yes, all algebraic functions in LISP must have a minimum of two arguments, except for the unary minus function.

How do you write the function that forms the sum of three or more quantities?

You write (Fig. 9):
(PLUS A B C)
which has the same meaning as:
(PLUS A(PLUS B C))

$$(\boxed{\text{PLUS}}\ \boxed{A}\ \boxed{B}\ \boxed{C})$$

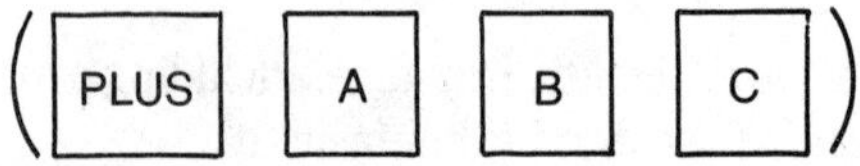

Fig. 9.

WHICH HAS THE SAME MEANING AS

$$(\boxed{\text{PLUS}}\ \boxed{A}\ (\boxed{\text{PLUS}}\ \boxed{B}\ \boxed{C}))$$

Does this procedure also apply to multiplication?

Yes, you can write X * Y * Z as (Fig. 10):
(TIMES X Y Z) instead of writing:
(TIMES X (TIMES Y Z))

$$(\boxed{\text{TIMES}}\ \boxed{X}\ \boxed{Y}\ \boxed{Z})$$

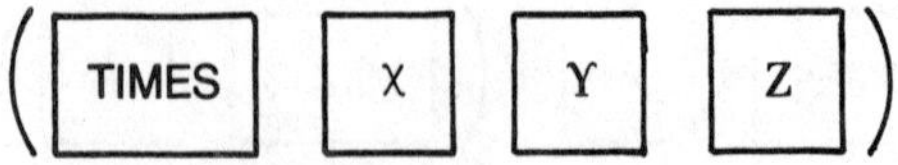

Fig. 10.

INSTEAD OF WRITING

$$(\boxed{\text{TIMES}}\ \boxed{X}\ (\boxed{\text{TIMES}}\ \boxed{Y}\ \boxed{Z}))$$

What are the arithmetic functions in LISP?

They are PLUS (addition), DIFFERENCE (subtraction), TIMES (multiplication), QUOTIENT (division) and REMAINDER (the value that remains after division).

What exactly is the REMAINDER function?

The REMAINDER function returns as its value the "remainder" when X is divided by Y. An example would be (Fig. 11):

(REMAINDER X Y)

if X and Y are 12 and 5 respectively, the remainder would be 2.

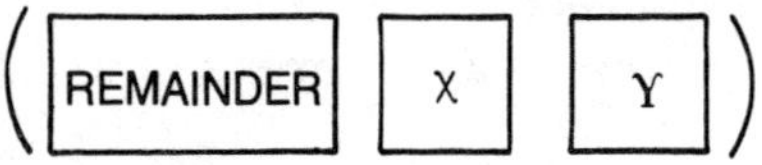

Fig. 11.

Are there any other mathematical functions available in LISP?

Yes, but they are discussed later.

EXPRESSIONS

Does the use of functions in LISP have disadvantages or advantages?

There are both disadvantages and advantages to the use of functions in the LISP manner.

What are the disadvantages?

The main disadvantages of the "function" method of LISP are the lengthier expressions and the need for more parentheses (Fig. 12). For example, it is certainly easier to write in BASIC:

SIN (X * X-4)*A/B

than it is to write in LISP:

(TIMES(SIN(DIFFERENCE(TIMES X X)4)) (QUOTIENT A B))

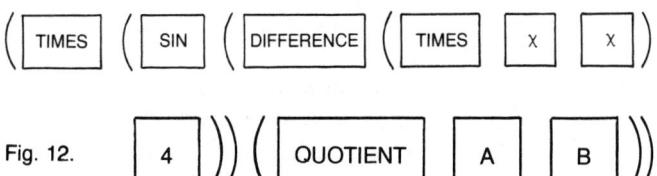

Fig. 12.

What are the advantages of functions?

The advantage of the functional notation in LISP is its ability to unify the language. In LISP, this is the only type of construction available. Every feature of LISP, such as the transferring of control, conditional tests, definitions and so forth are "defined" by creating a special function to handle them.

Is it always necessary to use all those parentheses for simple arithmetic?

Yes, for standard LISP. But there is a special version of LISP, called MLISP, which was designed to implement arithmetic functions without resorting to "all" those parentheses.

What are the expressions called that you have been using so far?

They are termed S-expressions.

How many component types are found in an S-expression?

Two, they are the "elements" such as numerics (1 2 3.....9) and character symbols (A B C . . . . Z). The other component is the parenthesis (Fig. 13).

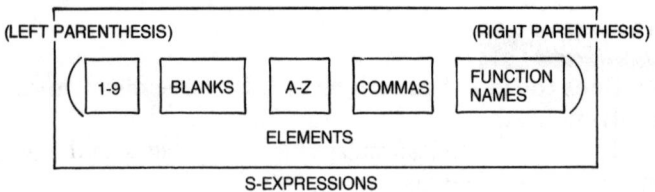

Fig. 13.

What do you call the numerics and symbols in LISP?

They are called ATOMS.

Is every expression that contains ATOMS and parentheses an S-expression?

No, an S-expression only exists if certain rules are followed.

Are the following examples S-expressions?

(TIMES V N))
)PLUS 4 5)
(DIFFERENCE A B)

The first two are not S-expressions because the first example ends in two parentheses and the second has a reversed first parenthesis. The third expression is indeed an S-expression.

How do you define an S-expression?

An S-expression is made up of ATOMS and parentheses. There must be a balance between the number of left parentheses and the number of right parentheses. There *must* be no reversal of parentheses and the parentheses *must not* be in the wrong spot.

14

Is there another important aspect of the S-expression?

Yes, you must also consider the blanks. In BASIC and in FORTRAN blanks are ignored. But in LISP blanks are very important to the operation of the functions.

What are blanks used for?

Blanks are used to separate arguments.

Can anything else be used instead of blanks in LISP?

Commas can be used instead, but most programmers prefer to use blanks.

In what ways can commas replace blanks?

A comma can be placed in any spot where a blank would have been (Fig. 14). The following examples will explain:

(TIMES C B)..........(TIMES, C B)
(TIMES C,B)
(TIMES,C,B)

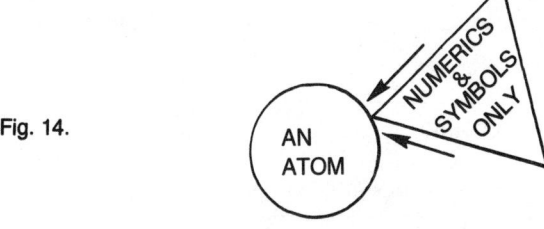

Fig. 14.

LIKE CLASSICAL PHYSICS, A LISP ATOM
CAN NOT BE DIVIDED TO ANYTHING SIMPLER

Can more than one blank be used in a given place and can blanks ever be left out?

In most programming languages, a string of blanks can be inserted anywhere providing at least one blank is required in the first place. Blanks can also be left out before or after a left or right parenthesis.

Are the following two S-expressions legal in LISP?

(TIMES (SIN (DIFFERENCE (TIMES X X) 4)) (QUOTIENT A B))

(TIMES (PLUS X C) H (PLUS A B) (PLUS R T))

Yes, they are both legal and acceptable in LISP. Only the number of blanks have been increased. The following S-expression is legal because only the blanks before the left and right parentheses have been removed:

(TIMES(PLUS X C) H(PLUS A B)(PLUS R T))

15

Can the above rules be applied with any function in LISP?

Yes, the rule applies to any construction in LISP.

ATOMS

What are the constants and variables in an S-expression called?

They are called ATOMS

What rules do variables follow in LISP?

Variables follow the standard rule for identifiers. They *must* be composed of letters or numbers and they *must* start with a letter only.

What is the difference between variables in LISP and in most other languages?

The major difference is in the upper amount of characters permitted in the variable name. Most languages only allow a certain amount of characters to be used. In LISP, any amount of characters can be used in the construction of a variable name (Fig. 15).

```
OTHER
LANGUAGES                    Fig. 15.
SHORT VARIABLE NAME
```

```
LISP       THIS IS A LONG VARIABLE NAME
```

Are there any special identifiers in LISP?

Yes, T, F and NIL.

What happens if you use one of these special (reserved) identifiers?

Typically, the results will be unpredictable.

What are these reserved variables or identifiers used for?

The T and F mean "true" and "false" respectively, while the NIL has a number of uses.

What are the uses of the NIL in LISP?

Most of the uses of NIL will be covered later, but one is worth mentioning now. Quite often in LISP, NIL is used to replace or substitute for F. Actually, F is not used very often to mean "false". NIL is used instead.

What is an ATOM?
An ATOM is any string of characters (Fig. 16).

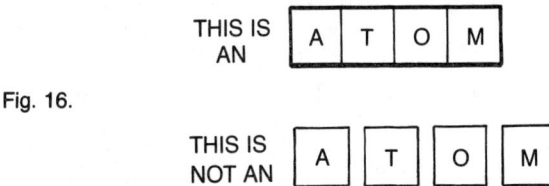

Fig. 16.

Can a variable have a value in LISP?
Yes, a variable in LISP, like in FORTRAN or BASIC, can have a value.

What is one way to give a variable a value in LISP?
You can use the SETQ function to assign a value to a variable.

What does a SETQ function look like and how does it operate?
The following is a valid SETQ function:
(SET Q Z 10)

The above S-expression sets the value of Z to 10. The first argument is the variable to be set and the second argument is the quantity to be placed there (Fig. 17).

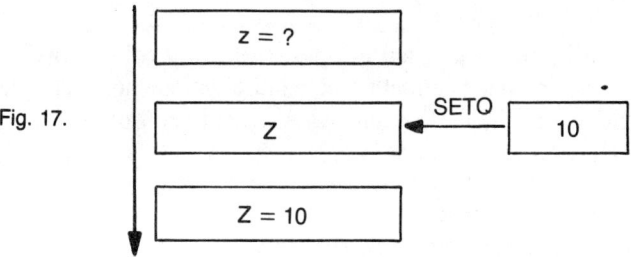

Fig. 17.

Can the second argument be more intricate that just a numeric quantity?
The second argument can be as involved as much as you like. The following are valid SETQ expressions:
(SETQ X Y)
(SETQ X (PLUS A B))
(SETQ X (DIFFERENCE A(TIMES C D)))

Are the SETQ expressions only used for numerics?
No, they can also be used with symbolics (Fig. 18).

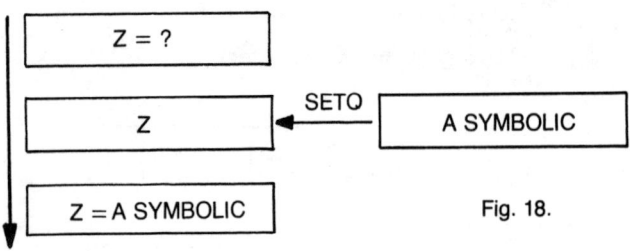

Fig. 18.

SYMBOLS

Besides being a "functional language" what else is LISP?

LISP is also a "symbolic" language. This means that one of its more important features is its ability to manipulate data that is not necessarily numbers.

What is a simple example of this ability?

Set the value of a variable, such as A, to be another ATOM, such as B. Note: this is quite different than setting A to B.

What does (SETQ A B) do?

The function:
(SETQ A B)
sets the A to the value of B. Therefore, if B had been set equal to 10,
then (SETQ A B) would set A equal to 10.

Does this expression operate in any other way?

Yes, if B had been set equal to J (the symbol, not what J stands for) then (SETQ A B) would set A equal to J (Fig. 19).

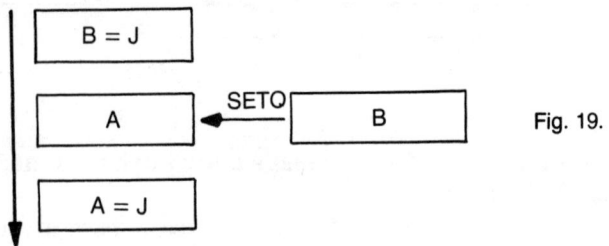

Fig. 19.

Is there another way to set symbols equal to other symbols?

Yes, you can use the QUOTE function of LISP.

If you wrote (SETQ A (QUOTE B)) what would happen?

A would be set equal to the symbol B.

Why?
Quote is a function whose value is its argument, therefore, the value of (QUOTE C) is "C".

What is the main differences between (SETQ A B) and (SETQ A (QUOTE B))?
The first S-expression:
(SETQ A B)
sets A equal to the value of B, while the second S-expression (Fig. 20).
(SETQ A (QUOTE B))

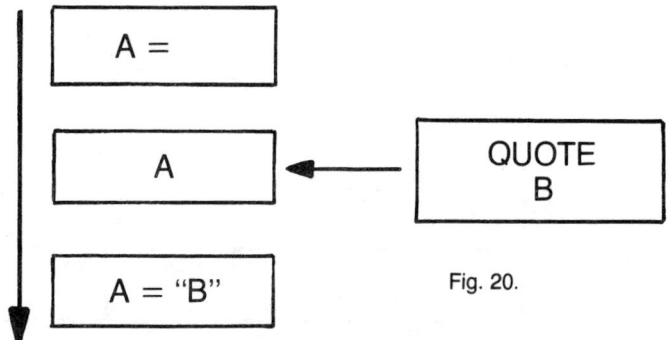

Fig. 20.

sets A equal to the value of (QUOTE B) which is B.

Is there another function similiar to SETQ in LISP?
Yes, it is called the SET function.

What does the SET function do?
In the S-expression (SET A B), the "value" of A is set to the "value" of B. This can be written as (Fig. 21):
(SET (QUOTE A) B).

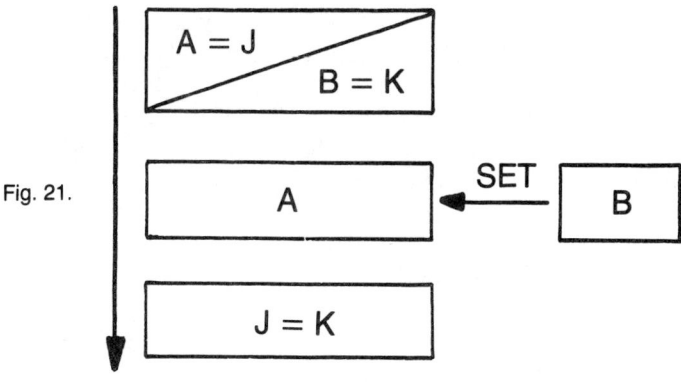

Fig. 21.

19

What happens if you use the SET function with variables that have ordinary numeric values?

You end up with results that are meaningless. Assume that A is equal to 10 and that B is equal to 20 and then write:
(SET A B)
You would be trying to set 10 equal to 20—which is obviously ridiculous.

When is SET used then?

If the value of A was the symbol K, then the function (Fig. 22).
(SET A B)
would set K equal to B.

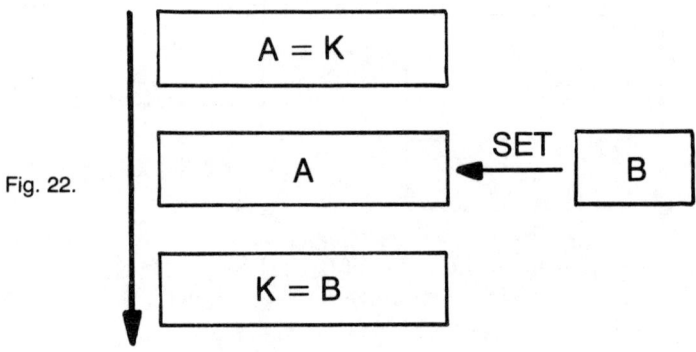

Fig. 22.

What is an important characteristic of numbers in LISP?

Every ATOM in LISP has a value. Every number that occurs in a LISP program is an ATOM and the value of these ATOMS are themselves.

Is this true for "symbolic" ATOMS as well?

No, generally in LISP, these characteristics of numbers do not apply to symbols. If you write in LISP:
(SETQ A 10)
you are setting A to the value of 10—which is 10 obviously! But if instead you write:
(SETQ A B)
you are setting A to the value of B. This is usually not (the symbol) B itself.

20

Do any "symbolic" variables always stand for themselves?

Yes, the No. 'T', 'F' and the special ATOM 'NIL.' The value of T, meaning "true", is "T" itself. The value of F meaning "false" is NIL and the value of NIL is "NIL."

When do you get meaningless results with numeric functions?

If the value of an ATOM is another ATOM with a "SYMBOLIC" name, the numeric functions will return worthless results. Obviously, it does not make sense to write:

(DIFFERENCE A B)

if the value of B is the symbol K. Functions that do operate on symbolic date will be discussed later.

LISTS

What is another type of data in the LISP language?
The "list" is another type of data.

If LISP is a symbolic-functional language, what else is it?

LISP is also a list processing language. Actually the name LISP, comes from LIST Processing.

What is a list in LISP?

A list is an order collection of data somewhat like an array (Fig. 23).

The following S-expression:
(CHEESE 2 3 4 HOUSE 67 GIRL)
is an S-expression of a list of 7 "elements."

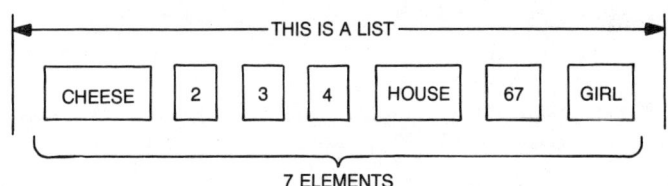

Fig. 23.

What is the difference between a list in LISP and an array in other languages?

A list in LISP can not be "indexed" in the way that an array can. If you want to refer or address the third item in the S-expression given (in this case, the number 3), you can not merely place the number 3 in an index register or its analog and expect to be able to get the third ATOM immediately. This is a result of the way in which ATOMS on a LIST (or references to them) are "chained" together.

How are ATOMS chained together?

Each and every ATOM or reference has a pointer, associated with it that points to the next reference (Fig. 24). This clearly means that the addresses of the various ATOMS and references are not in "sequence" in the way they would be in an array, such as in BASIC or FORTRAN. More detail on this later!

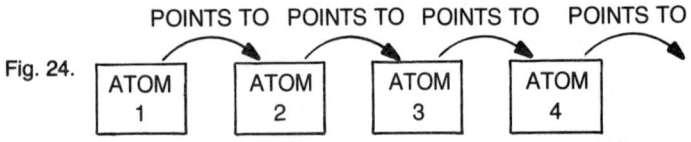

Fig. 24.

What happens if you write (SETQ A (CHEESE 234 HOUSE 67 GIRL))?

You are trying to set A equal to the above mentioned LIST and you run into problems (Fig. 25).

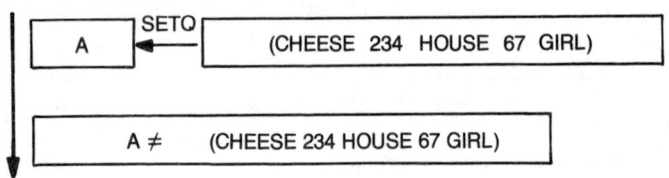

Fig. 25.

What sort of problems arise from this form of manipulation?

Take the example:
(SETQ A (DIFFERENCE B C))

It is obvious that you want to set A equal to B-C. What you do not want to do is to set A equal to the "LIST" DIFFERENCE B C. Therefore, a convention which always holds in LISP was developed (Fig. 26).

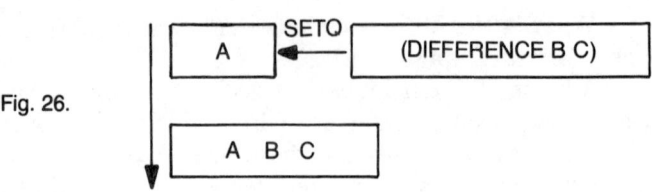

Fig. 26.

What is this "convention"?
Whenever an expression (such as (DIFFERENCE B C)) appears inside an S-expression, the "first" ATOM encountered (in this example it is DIFFERENCE) is taken to specify a function. The remaining ATOMS are understood to be arguments of that function. Obviously, this applies to "layered" parentheses (parentheses within parentheses) as well. If a subexpression occurs, the first ATOM "again" is taken as the function—and so on (Fig. 27).

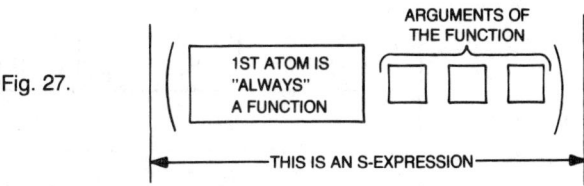

Fig. 27.

The problem is still not clear. What is it?
In the first example:
(SETQ A(CHEESE 234 HOUSE 67 GIRL))
the first ATOM in the subexpression is CHEESE and LISP would see CHEESE as being a function. Since there is no function named CHEESE, the LISP operating system would report an error!

Then how do you write (SETQ A(CHEESE 234 HOUSE 67 GIRL)) so that it is a legal expression?
Use the QUOTE function (Fig. 28). If you wrote:
(SETQ A(QUOTE(CHEESE 234 HOUSE 67 GIRL)))
You would not have any problems. In the QUOTE function and only in the QUOTE function the rule of "first" ATOM is not followed.

The ATOM CHEESE is not taken as being a function name. The value of the QUOTE function in this example, as in any usage of QUOTE, is the argument of the QUOTE function *just as it stands* (it is understood to be a literal string).

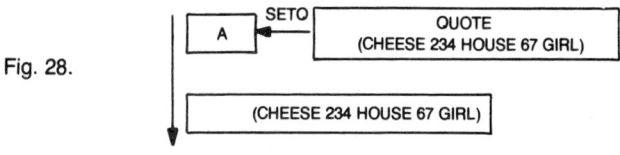

Fig. 28.

23

Is there another way to produce a list as the value of a function?

Yes, by using the LIST function (Fig. 29). Therefore, the value of:

(LIST CHEESE GIRL)

is (CHEESE GIRL). This result is obviously the same as the value of:

((QUOTE(CHEESE GIRL))

but there is a difference between the LIST and QUOTE functions.

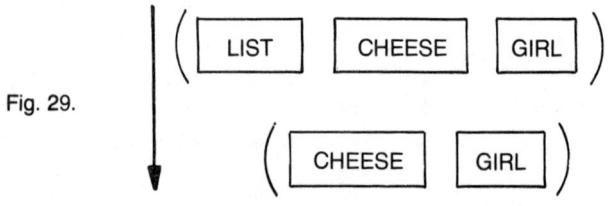

Fig. 29.

What are the differences between LIST and QUOTE?

If the arguments are symbolic, there is indeed a great difference between LIST and QUOTE (Fig. 30). Assume that A is set to 3 then:

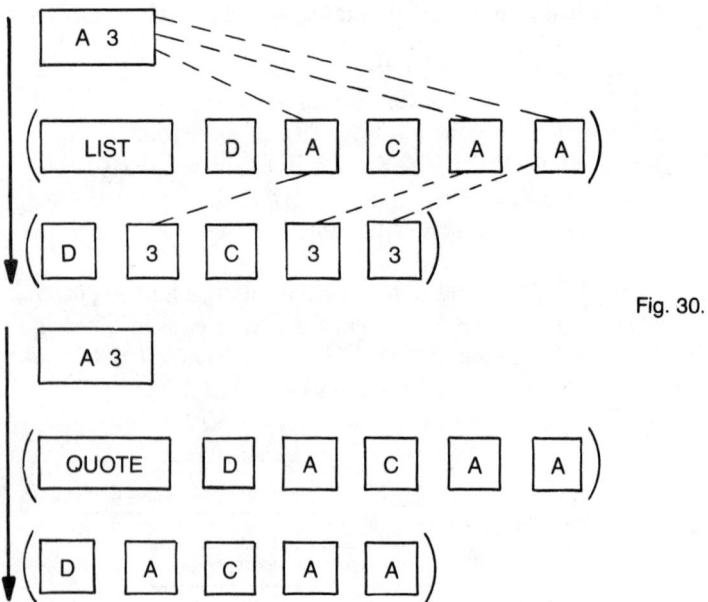

Fig. 30.

(LIST D A C A A)
has the value of:
(D 3 C 3 3)
but if you had used the QUOTE function instead to write:
(QUOTE(D A C A A))
you would have the value of:
(D A C A A).

Can any function have as its value a list?

Yes, in particular, there is one function that is an arithmetic value that has as its value a list of two ATOMS. This function is DIVIDE and its list is the quotient and the remainder. Therefore:

(DIVIDE 3 5 4)

has as its value the list (8 3). However, such a list can not be used directly by the arithmetic functions, even *if* it would contain only one "element." Therefore, you can easily see that (DIFFERENCE S 6) is absolutely meaningless—and will cause a LISP system error—if S is the LIST (7), although it is equal to 1 if S was the ATOM 7.

SUBLISTS

What is the result of the elements being chained together in memory?

Because of the way the chaining takes place, it is possible for the elements of a list to be either ATOMS or sublists.

What is a sublist in LISP?

A sublist is simply a list contained within another list (Fig. 31). For example, you might want to construct a list of four

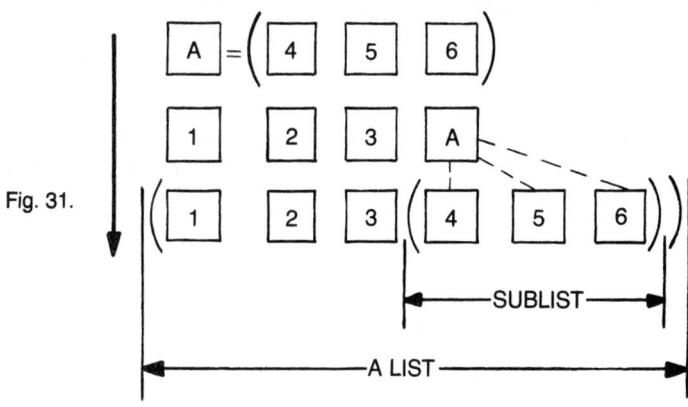

Fig. 31.

elements or items, 1 2 3 and A, and where A stands for another list of 3 elements, 4 5 and 6. For this case write:
(1 2 3(4 5 6))
as the S-expression for this list. Of course the sublists of a list can also contain sublists, and so on ad infinitum.

What is the relation between LISP as a "list processing" language and as a functional language?

The function expressions, or S-expressions, which specify function calls in LISP also specify lists. Therefore, the following example:
(SETQ A(PLUS B (TIMES C 10)))
is a list of three elements. The first element is SETQ, the second is A, and the third is also a list of three elements. These three elements are PLUS, B and the third is another three element list containing TIMES, C and 10.

How does a function reference in LISP appear in memory?

It appears in memory as a list. Whenever an S-expression such as (DIFFERENCE X Y) occurs anywhere within a LISP program that has been entered into memory, a list is formed. In this case the list of three elements are DIFFERENCE, X and Y.

Normally, what is the first element of these lists?

The first element of such a list will normally be an ATOM since it stands for a function. However, there are some cases in which a sublist can be used in this position to specify a function.

What are the remaining "elements" called?

The elements following the first are either ATOMS or sublists. A sublist in this position specifies a function inside the original function.

How is a function represented in memory?

A function reference is represented as a "list" in memory.

What is the general rule about lists and S-expressions?

As a general rule, "to every S-expression in LISP there corresponds a list and to every list in LISP there corresponds an S-expression."(Fig. 32).

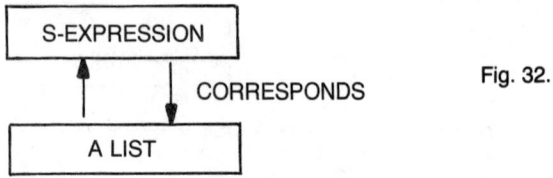

Fig. 32.

26

RECURSION

Besides being a "symbolic functional list processing language" what else is LISP?

LISP is also a recursive language.

Is LISP recursive like ALGOL?

In ALGOL, there are functions that do indeed call themselves—either directly or indirectly (Fig. 33). If the function "X" contains within its structure a call to itself, then that X calls itself directly. If a function X calls another function labelled C and the second function C calls X, then X calls itself indirectly.

Fig. 33.
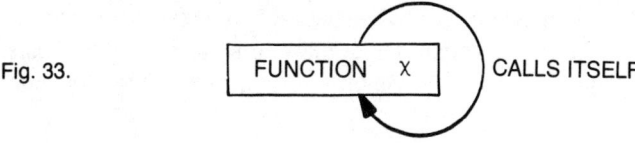
CALLS ITSELF

Can this be stated more generally?

Yes, if there are several fuctions in ALGOL named $Z_1, Z_2, Z_3 \ldots$, such that Z_1 calls Z_{i+1} for $1 \leq i < n$, and Z_n calls Z_1, then that Z_1 calls itself indirectly (and for that matter so do all the other Z_i) (Fig. 34).

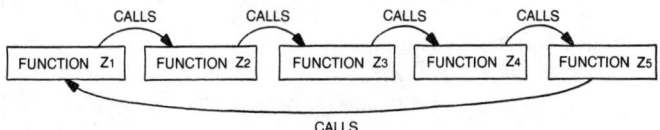

Fig. 34.

Is this the same with the LISP language?

In LISP, a function you have defined can in fact be recursive like the functions in ALGOL, but in LISP you also use the concept of recursive function as it is defined in "LOGIC."

What is a "circular" definition?

Take the example of "factorials." When you use the standard definition of factorial, the factorial of n to be n multiplied by the factorial of n-1, you are making a circular definition. You are defining a function by using a definition which includes the function itself. Typically this would make the "idea" of the definition improper. In the example of "factorial," if you specify or define that factorial 0 is 1, the definition does give the value of the factorial of any positive integer.

27

How do you name functions that seem to be "circular"?

Definitions which seem to be circular, but in fact specify a function uniquely over a certain range, are called definitions of a recursive function.

Can a function have more than one definition?

Yes, many functions have both ordinary definitions plus recursive definitions.

Can this idea of recursiveness help define the S-expression?

Yes, you can now use a recursive definition for the S-expression. An S-expression is either an ATOM or it is a left parenthesis followed by a sequence of S-expressions separated either by blanks or commas and followed by a right parenthesis. The S-expressions in the sequence can also be ATOMS or other sequences. For example:

((A B)C((D E) F))

This S-expression consists of a left parenthesis followed by the sequence of S-expressions (A B), C, ((D E)F) followed by a right parenthesis. Each of these sequences themselves can be defined to be S-expressions in the same way.

Using the recursive definitions what is a LIST?

A list is a sequence of references, each of which can be a reference to an ATOM or another list (Fig. 35). In reference to this recursive definition of a list, it is important to remember that a list is not a sequence of ATOMS. The dividing line in definitions here become quite fine, but they are quite important in LISP. An ATOM is represented in memory by an item which includes its name and which can also include various properties of the ATOM. A list that includes this atom *only* "includes" the pointer to that atom.

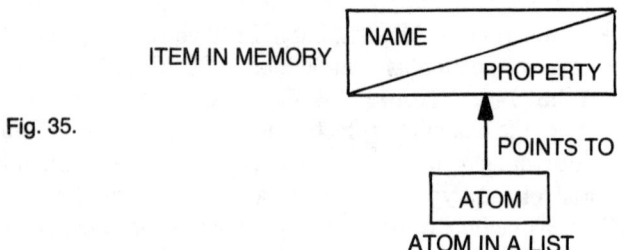

Fig. 35.

What is the definition of a list then?

A list in LISP is a list of pairs. One member of the pair is the pointer to an ATOM while the other is a pointer to the next pair (Fig. 36).

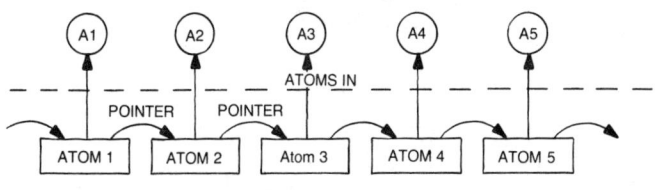

Fig. 36.

THE LISP SYSTEM

What is the LISP operating system?

Most LISP systems allow you to make some early experiments without worrying about functions of programs. Of course, you can use the "standard" built in functions such as SIN, COS DIFFERENCE, PLUS and others.

Is the operation of the LISP system like FORTRAN?

No, normally FORTRAN is considered to be a compiler. The source program is entered into the system and the FORTRAN compiler compiles or creates an "object" program. It is this object program that is actually executed when you run a FORTRAN program. In LISP, an interpreter is used. A function is entered into the LISP system and its value is calculated immediately. This is not to say that compilers do not exist for LISP as well. This will be discussed later.

Considering how the interpreter system works, what can you do with it?

Since you have not learned how to program in LISP yet, I will discuss the basic ideas and how to do simple functions. If you type (using a teletype, decwriter or similar tele-printer):

TIMES (5 6)

The computer would respond with:

30.

The line you just typed seems to be wrong. Why does it work?

The LISP system reads not just one S-expression at a time but two S-expressions at a time (Fig. 37). The first S-expression specifies a function, while the second S-expression specifies its arguments. Therefore, when the LISP system reads TIMES (5 6), it is actually reading two S-expressions. The first S-expression is

29

the function TIMES and the second S-expression is its arguments 5 6. It is plain to see that TIMES (5 6) can be derived from the proper expression (TIMES 5 6) as follows. Remove the first left parenthesis and place it forward so that it appears *after* the first element of the S-expression instead of before it. This creates a short cut.

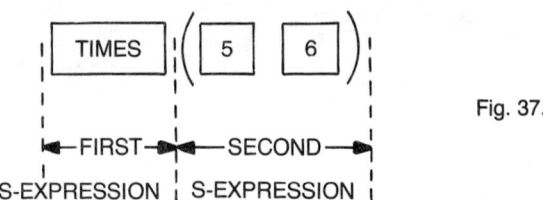

Fig. 37.

Will this short cut work with other, or even all, functions?

No, if you take the example of:
TIMES (5 PLUS (6 7))
as an input line to the LISP system, the interpreter would signal an input error.

Why?

The list (5 PLUS (6 7)) is a list of three quantities—the integer 5, the symbol PLUS and the list (6 7). Therefore, the form PLUS (6 7) can not be used inside another pair of parentheses. See "what is this convention?" in the section on lists.

When can you use this short cut?

Use it with the following modification. Whenever you use a function at the "top" level (not enclosed by parentheses), you can use a format like TIMES (5 6) or in general "FUNCTION" (A B). But whenever you use a function that is not at the top level—in other words it is buried in parentheses—you must use the conventional format of (FUNCTION A B).

Is there more about this TOP level concept?

Yes, the top level is merely a special case of the concept of the parentheses levels (Fig. 38). Any ATOM within an S-expression

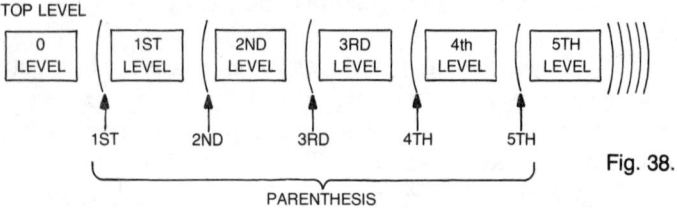

Fig. 38.

30

which is at some parentheses level can be defined as being at the nth level. If it is outside the parentheses it is at the "0th" level.

Can any of the LISP functions covered so far work at the 0 level?

Yes, all will work at the 0 level except for the SETQ function. On this function systems must be on level 1 or greater.

What would some examples be if you consider only 0 level?

You can write:
TIMES (5 6)
30
DIFFERENCE (45 30)
15
PLUS (23 34)
57
QUOTIENT (10 2)
5
REMAINDER (11 2)
1

It is self-evident that the numbers following the above examples are the solutions or results to the S-expressions entered into the LISP system.

Are there functions without any arguments?

Yes, functions do exist without arguments, even though they have not been mentioned yet.

How would you write such a function using the shortcut in LISP?

Assuming you had a function called AABBCC, you could write:

AABBCC( ).

What does the symbol ( ) stand for?

The symbols ( ) stand for an empty list (a list that contains no items).

Is there another way to denote an empty list?

Yes, you can produce an empty list by writing NIL. As mentioned earlier, NIL has several meanings in LISP.

How would you use the NIL symbol?

Write using our imaginary function AABBCC:
AABBCC NIL
which has the same identical meaning as:
AABBCC( )

SUBEXPRESSIONS

Can you write more complex functions, still using the interpreter, without programming?

Yes, assume that you want to write the expression:
(TIMES(DIFFERENCE 20 10) (PLUS 5 5))
You would hope the system would respond with the answer 100. But as discussed earlier, you can not simply write or type in this functional expression and expect it to work.

Why?

Because TIMES is a function at the top level. On most LISP interpreter systems, there is another reason why you can not merely type:
TIMES(DIFFERENCE 20 10) (PLUS 5 5))
even though in the last section it seemed that you could. This is because the *convention* (mentioned earlier) that covers the evaluation of functions inside other functions is not followed when you are dealing with a function at the 0 level of parentheses. The line is equivalent to multiplying the LIST (DIFFERENCE 20 10) by the LIST (PLUS 5 5) and not the numbers 20-10 and 5 + 5. The TIMES function operates on numbers and not on LISTS. Therefore, a system working error will be generated by the LISP interpreter.

How can these expressions be evaluated?

One way to circumvent this problem is to use the function EVAL. If A is any S-expression involving integers, such as the example given in the second paragraph of this section, you construct the input line to be typed as EVAL(A). Some LISP systems use different varieties of EVAL. They are:
EVAL(A)
EVAL(A NIL)
or
EVAL (A)
to find or evaluate an expression. Since A is contained in parentheses, it is not necessary (and would be *wrong*) to move the first parenthesis to the right of the function name as discussed in the section on the LISP system. Therefore, to evaluate the expression:
(TIMES(DIFFERENCE 20 10)(PLUS 5 5))
type in:
EVAL((TIMES(DIFFERENCE 20 10)(PLUS 5 5)))
and the system will respond with 100.

Is there another method of evaluating functions similar to the use of the function EVAL?

Yes, you can use the (LAMBDA NIL A) NIL. This method works on all LISP systems regardless of type.

How to you use the LAMBDA function?

To evaluate the expression described two steps earlier using the LAMBDA function, type in:

(LAMBDA NIL(TIMES(DIFFERENCE 20 10)(PLUS 5 5)))NIL

this of course will return the value of 100.

How extensive is the LAMBDA function with reference to any function?

Any arithmetic S-expression you want to choose can be evaluated using the LAMBDA function, regardless of the complexity of the S-expression involved.

What about extra parentheses in LISP?

No!, it should be readily seen and easily understood that extra parentheses cannot be inserted without a specific purpose (Fig. 39).

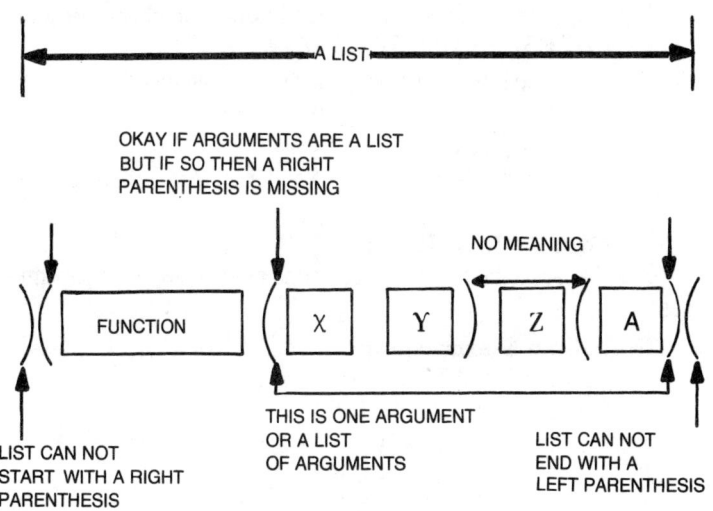

Fig. 39.

What about EVAL((PLUS(8) (DIFFERENCE 34 25))). Will it run?

No, it would definitely be incorrect because the (8) would imply that the 8 was a function without arguments (Fig. 40).

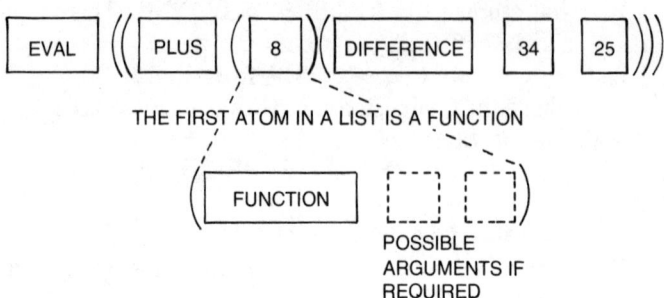

Fig. 40.

FIRST REVIEW

Is CHEESE an ATOM?
Yes, because CHEESE is a string of characters.
Is 9876 an ATOM?
Yes, because 9876 is a string of characters.
Is K an ATOM?
Yes, because K is a string of characters, one character long.
Is (CHEESE IS GOOD) a LIST?
Yes, because it is a collection of ATOMS enclosed in parentheses.
Is (GIRL) a LIST?
Yes, because GIRL is an ATOM and it is enclosed in parentheses.
Is ((MICE ARE)NICE) a LIST?
Yes, because the two S-expressions now enclosed in parentheses.
IS ABC an S-expression?
Yes, because all ATOMS are S-expressions.
Is (A B C) an S-expression?
Yes, because it is a LIST.
IS (A(B)C) an S-expression?
Yes, because all LISTS are S-expressions.
How many S-expressions are in this list (MICE ARE NICE)?
Three MICE, ARE, NICE.
Is ( ) a LIST?
Yes, because it is a collection of zero S-expressions enclosed in parentheses. This is a special S-expression called the NULL LIST.

Is this a LIST (() () ())?

Yes, because it is a collection of S-expressions enclosed in parentheses.

How do you write 4COSA-6 in LISP?

(DIFFERENCE (TIMES 4(COS A)) 6)

How do we write $A^2/B^3 - \sqrt{}^2$ in LISP?

(QUOTIENT(TIMES A A) (DIFFERENCE(TIMES B B B) (TIMES V V)))

What does (TIMES A S D (MINUS F)) mean in LISP?

A*S*D*-F or if you wish A*S*D*(-F)

What does (REMAINDER A B) mean in LISP?

This function returns the remainder when A is divided by B.

Are the following examples S-expressions?

(TIMES(MINUS B)(MINUS C)
(PLUS A C H T R))
(QUOTIENT)PLUS A B)(DIFFERENCE G H))
(REMAINDER (PLUS A B C D)(TIMES F G H))

The first three are not valid S-expressions, but the last one is. The first expression has one right parenthesis missing at the end of the expression. The second expression has one too many right parentheses at the end of the expression. The third expression has its second "left" parenthesis reversed.

Write the following assignment statement in LISP notation.

R equal to (P-T)/(Y2)

(SETQ R (QUOTIENT(DIFFERENCE P T)(TIMES Y Y))))

At this point, is there anything that has not been covered?

If there are any doubts in your mind about the material covered, read the sections that deal with that material.

FUNCTIONS IN LISP

What does the word DEFINE mean in LISP?

The word or symbol DEFINE means that following it is a function definition.

Is DEFINE a "function"?

Yes, as stated before, LISP is only constructed of functions and no other type of constructions.

Does DEFINE have an analog in FORTRAN?

Yes, the function DEFINE is somewhat like the FORTRAN word *function*. But, the word DEFINE in LISP is a function and the word function in FORTRAN is a *keyword*.

35

What are the arguments of the function DEFINE?

DEFINE has only one argument and it is a list of functions that are to be defined. Each function that is to be defined is itself a list of two *elements*. The first of these elements is the function name and the second element is the function definition or description. Therefore, write:

DEFINE(((AAAz$_1$) (BBBz$_2$) (CCCz$_3$)))

where z$_1$, z$_2$ and z$_3$ stand for the three function descriptions or definitions in this example. This example would define three functions AAA, BBB and CCC respectively (Fig. 41). The expression (((AAAz$_1$) (BBBz$_2$) (CCCz$_3$))) is the list of arguments of DEFINE.

But, there is only one argument for DEFINE. Actually, ((AAAz$_1$) (BBBz$_2$) (CCCz$_3$)) is a single argument. Therefore, the definition of DEFINE still holds.

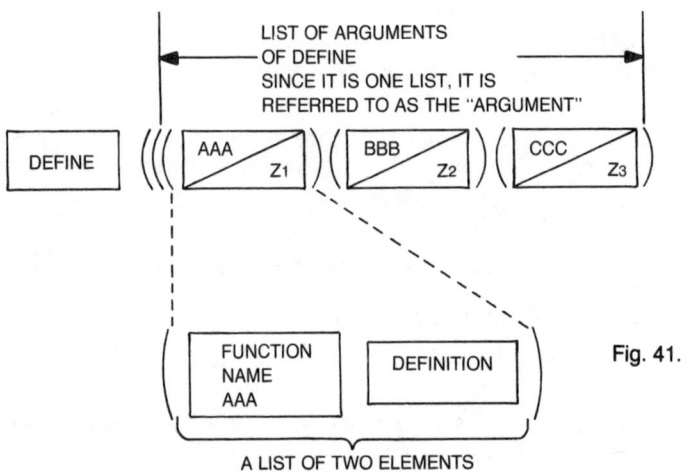

Fig. 41.

But there are three functions to be defined. How can this be only one argument?

This is because the argument itself is written as a list of three S-expressions. Note that in the example given, AAA, BBB and CCC stand for, or are taken to mean that they stand for, the names AAA, BBB and CCC and not the quantities that AAA, BBB and CCC stand for.

What are the legal specifications for a function definition in LISP?

Any legal specification of a previously known function can be used in the construction or definition of new functions in LISP when using the DEFINE function.

What does the following expression represent?
DEFINE (((AAA PLUS)(BBB REMAINDER)(CCC QUOTIENT)))

You have defined AAA to have the same function as PLUS, that BBB will have the same function as REMAINDER and that CCC will have the same function as QUOTIENT (Fig. 42). Therefore, if you write:

(AAA C B)

You are summing C and B together the same as if you used the expression:

(PLUS C B)

or

(BBB R T)

You are finding the remainder from the division of R by T which is the same as the expression:

(REMAINDER R T)

or

(CCC 4 2)

You are finding the quotient of 4 and 2 when 4 is divided by 2. This is the same as if you used the *standard* function QUOTIENT:

(QUOTIENT 4 2).

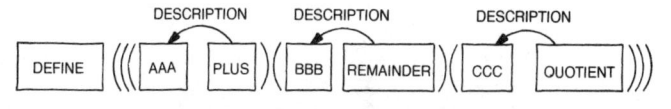

THE SECOND ELEMENT DESCRIBES THE FIRST

Fig. 42.

Can you combine these functions?
Yes, once a function has been defined it acts like any other function and can be used as such.

Can you write a more complex expression using the functions AAA, BBB and CCC?
Assuming that AAA stands for plus, BBB stands for REMAINDER and CCC stands for QUOTIENT, you can write:

(BBB(CCC(AAA 44 2) (AAA 1 1))7)

which has the same result as the expression:

(REMAINDER (QUOTIENT (PLUS 44 2) (PLUS 1 1))7)

and both of them, being identical in operation or function, return the value of 2 (Fig. 43).

When using the DEFINE function, what is very important?

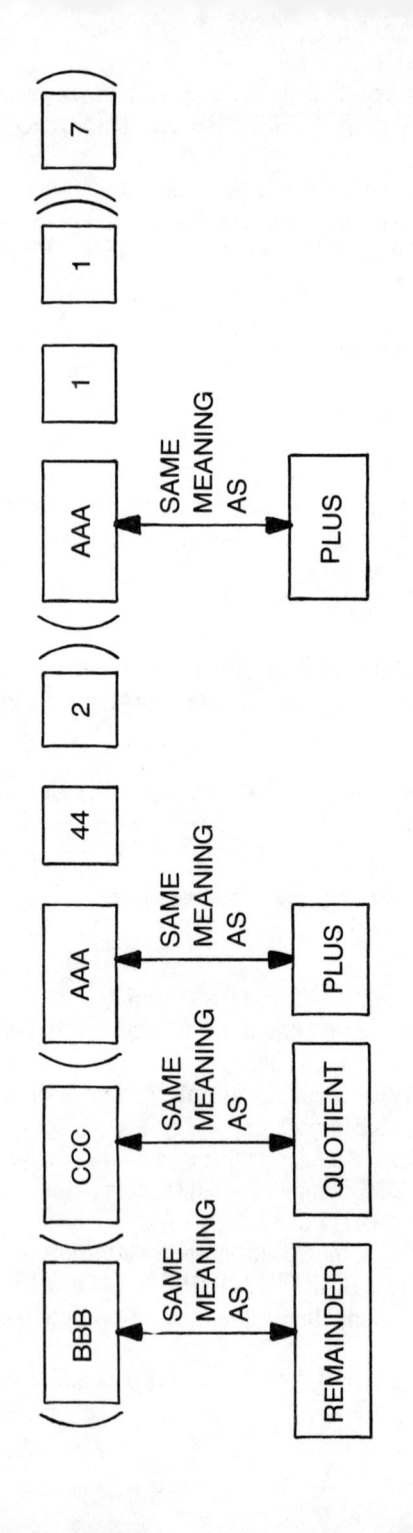

Fig. 43.

It is evident that you can only define new functions with the standard functions and with functions that have been previously defined.

COMMON LISP FUNCTIONS

Use the following notations with the list of common LISP functions, definitions and examples:

A....ATOM
B....Body of the Program
F....FUNCTION
L....LIST
NIL..False
S....S-expression
T....True
X....NUMBER
AR (can be any of the above)....ARGUMENT

Notations are numbered as follows: 1 is the first position, 2 is the second position in a LIST and the notation 1....n stands for any number of arguments of the class specified by the letter preceeding it.

function	definition	example
ABS	Returns the absolute value of its argument	(ABS X)
ADD1	Returns the argument plus one.	(ADD1 X)
AND	Returns NIL if any of the S-expressions are NIL and returns T otherwise	(AND...S...S..) (Fig. 44)
APPEND	Returns a single list whose elements are the elements of the two lists that were its arguments.	(APPEND L1 L2)
APPLY	Operates on the arguments with the function given as if that function appeared first in the S-expression.	(APPLY F AR)
ASSOC	Uses its first argument as a key and looks for that same key in the list that is the second argument. The value of ASSOC is the entire element whose CAR matches the key. If the key is not found the value is NIL.	(ASSOC A L)

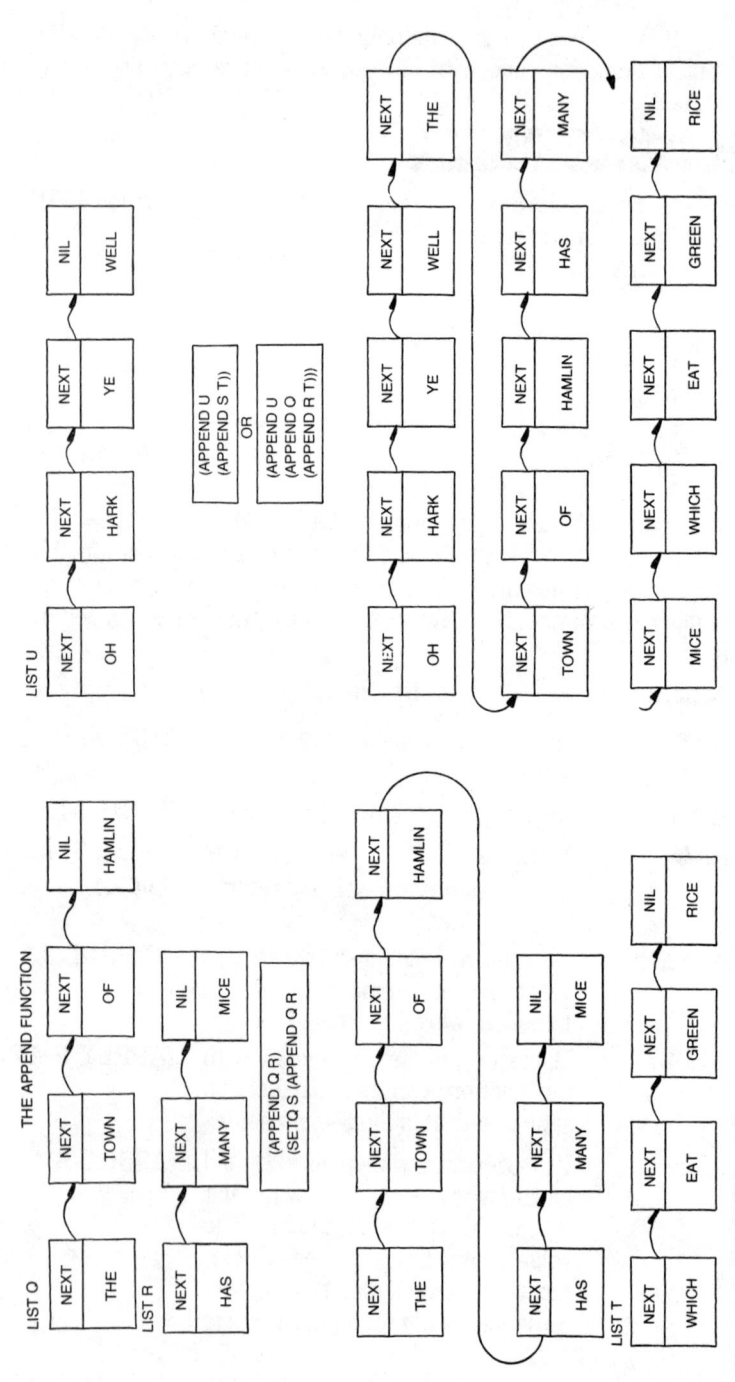

Fig. 44. The APPEND Function.

function	definition	example
ATOM	Returns T if the S-expression is an ATOM, if not it returns NIL.	(ATOM S)
CAR	Returns the first element of a list.	(CAR L) (Fig. 45)
CDR	Returns the list with the first element removed.	(CDR L) (Fig. 48)
COND	The LISP branching function.	(COND L1 L2 Ln)
	Adds the S-expression to the given list as the first element.	(CONS S L) (Fig. 49)
DEFINE	Defines a function, the function name is the value returned.	(DEFINE F AR1 ..ARn...B)
DEFPROP	Installs the S-expression as the given property of the atom.	(DEFPROP A S P)
DELETE	Removes the occurnces of the S-expression which appear as elements of a list. The number removed is determined by the third argument. If not present, all occurrences are removed.	(DELETE S L X) (Fig. 50)
DIFFERENCE	Returns the first argument minus the second argument.	(DIFFERENCE X X)
DO	The iteration function in LISP	DO
EQUAL	Returns T if the S-expressions are "IDENTICAL".	(EQUAL S S)
EVAL	Returns the value of the evaluated S-expression.	(EVAL S)
EXPLODE	Returns a list of single character atoms from the atom given.	(EXPLODE A) (Fig. 51)
EXP	Raises e to the power indicated.	(EXP X)
EXPT	Raises the first argument to the power indicated by the second argument.	(EXPT X X)
FUNCALL	Operates on the arguments with the function given (somewhat like APPLY).	(FUNCALL F ARL...ARn)

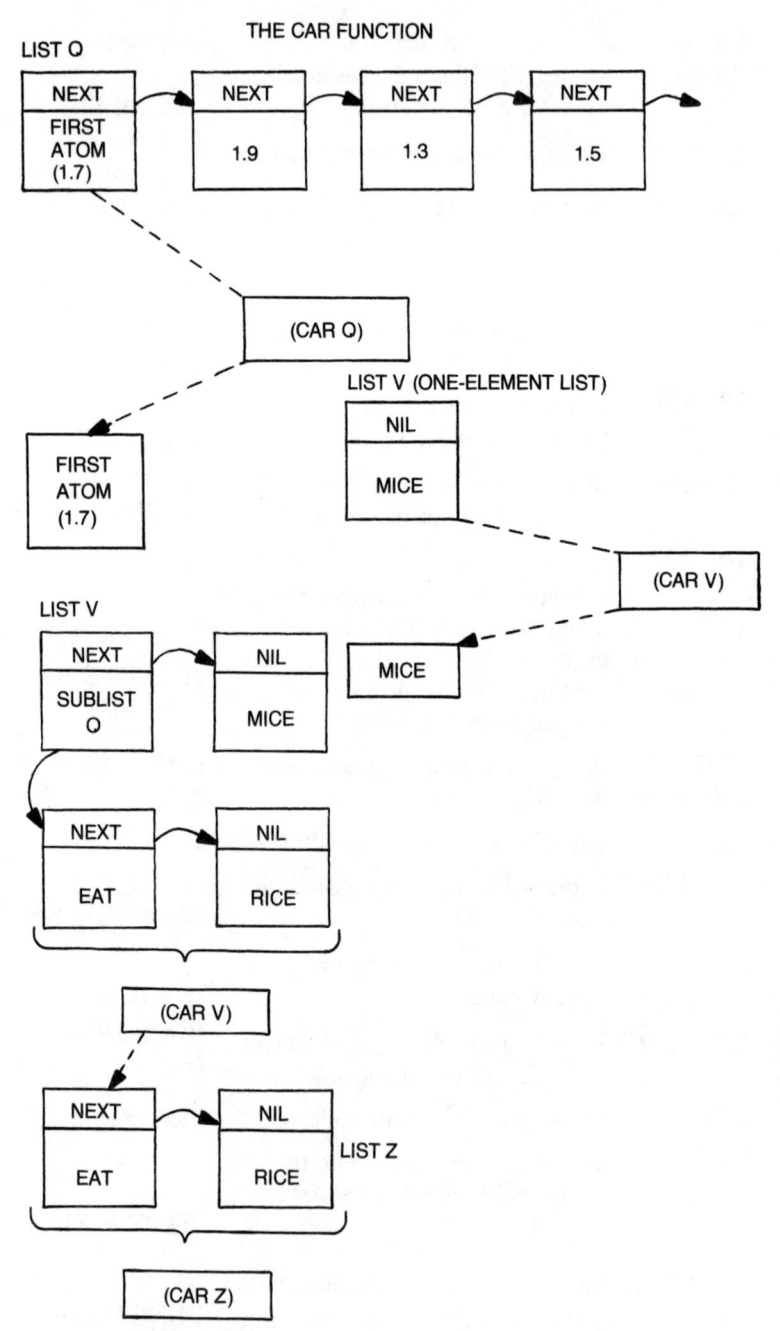

Fig. 45. The CAR Function.

42

function	definition	example
GET	Returns the value of the named property associated with the atom.	**(GET A P)**
GO	Unconditional branching.	**(GO T)**
GREATERP	Returns T if all the arguments are in decreasing order.	**(GREATERP X1...Xn)**
IMPLODE	Forms the single characters given in a list into an atom.	**(IMPLODE L)** (Fig. 52)
LAMBDA	Somewhat like define.	**(LAMBDA AR B)**
LAST	Returns the list with all the elements before the last one was removed.	**(LAST L)**
LENGTH	Returns the number of elements in a list.	**(LENGTH L)** (Fig. 53)

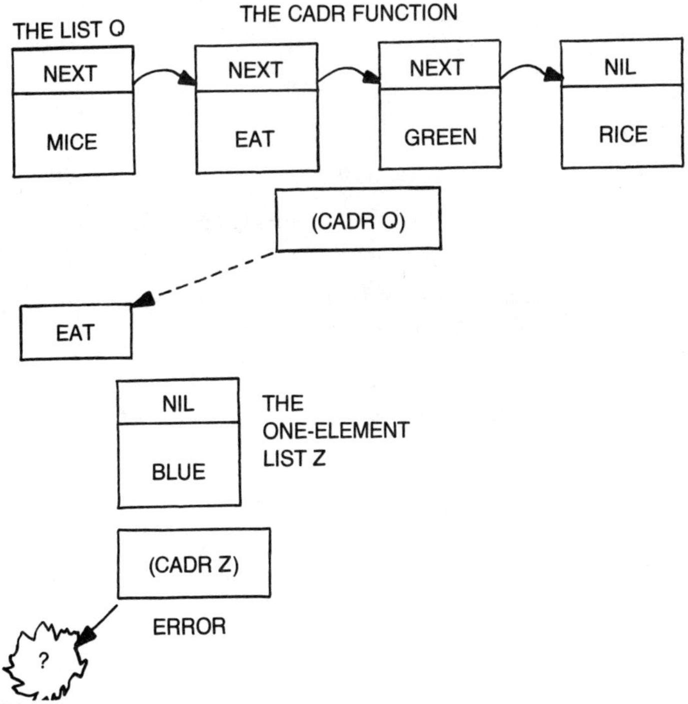

MEMBER

Fig. 46. The CADR Function.

43

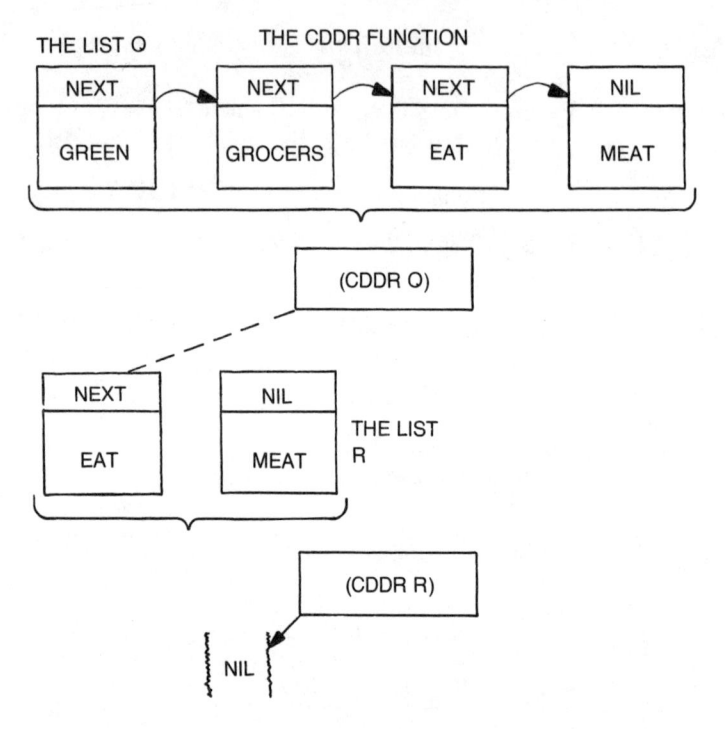

Fig. 47. The CDDR Function.

function	definition	example
LESSP	Returns T if all the arguments are in increasing order.	**(LESSP X1...Xn)** (Fig. 54)
LIST	Returns a list of n elements constructed from the n elements.	**(LIST S1...Sn)** (Fig. 55)
MAPCAR	Applies a function to a list or list of arguments. Returns a list of the results.	**(MAPCAR F AR1..ARn)** (Fig. 56)
MAX	Returns the Largest argument.	**(MAX X1 . . Xn)** (Fig. 57)
	Returns T if the S-expression is equal to a top-level (0-level) element of the list.	**(MEMBER S L)**
MIN	Returns the smallest argument.	**(MIN X1..Xn)** (Fig. 58)

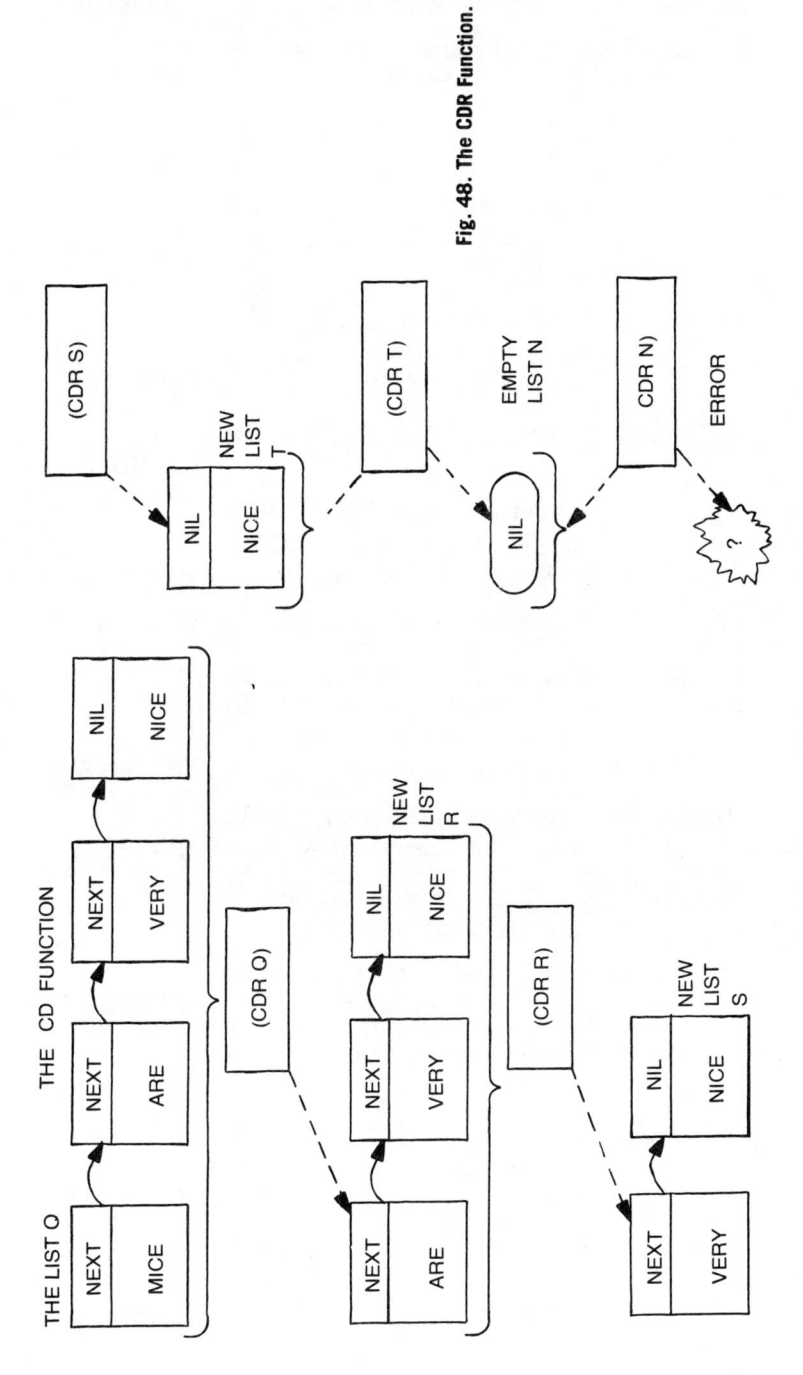

Fig. 48. The CDR Function.

function	definition	example
MINUS	Returns the unary minus (negative) of the argument.	(MINUS X)
MINUSP	Returns T if the argument is negative.	(MINUSP X)
NOT	Returns T if the S-expression is NIL or NIL is anything else (same as NULL).	(NOT S)
NULL	Returns T if the S-expression is an empty list or NIL if it is anything else (same as NOT).	(NULL S)
NUMBERP	Returns T if the argument is a number.	(NUMBERP S)
OR	Returns the value of T if at least one S-expression is non-NIL. Otherwise it returns NIL.	(OR S1..Sn)
PLUS	Adds all the arguments together.	(PLUS X1..Xn)
PLUSP	Returns T if the argument is positive	(PLUSP X)
PRINC	like PRINT, except print issues a carriage return before starting and a space when finished.	(PRINC S)
PRINT	Causes the S-expression to be printed, the value is always T.	(PRINT S)
PROG	See text — creates variables and supports iteration.	
PUTPROP	Installs the S-expression as the given property of the atom.	(PUTPROP
QUOTE	Is complete the same as the 'S-expression.	(QUOTE S)
QUOTIENT	Returns the result of dividing the first argument by the second argument.	(QUOTIENT X X)
READ	Causes the S-expression to be returned as the value of the PROG it appears in.	(RETURN S)

Fig. 49. The CONS Function.

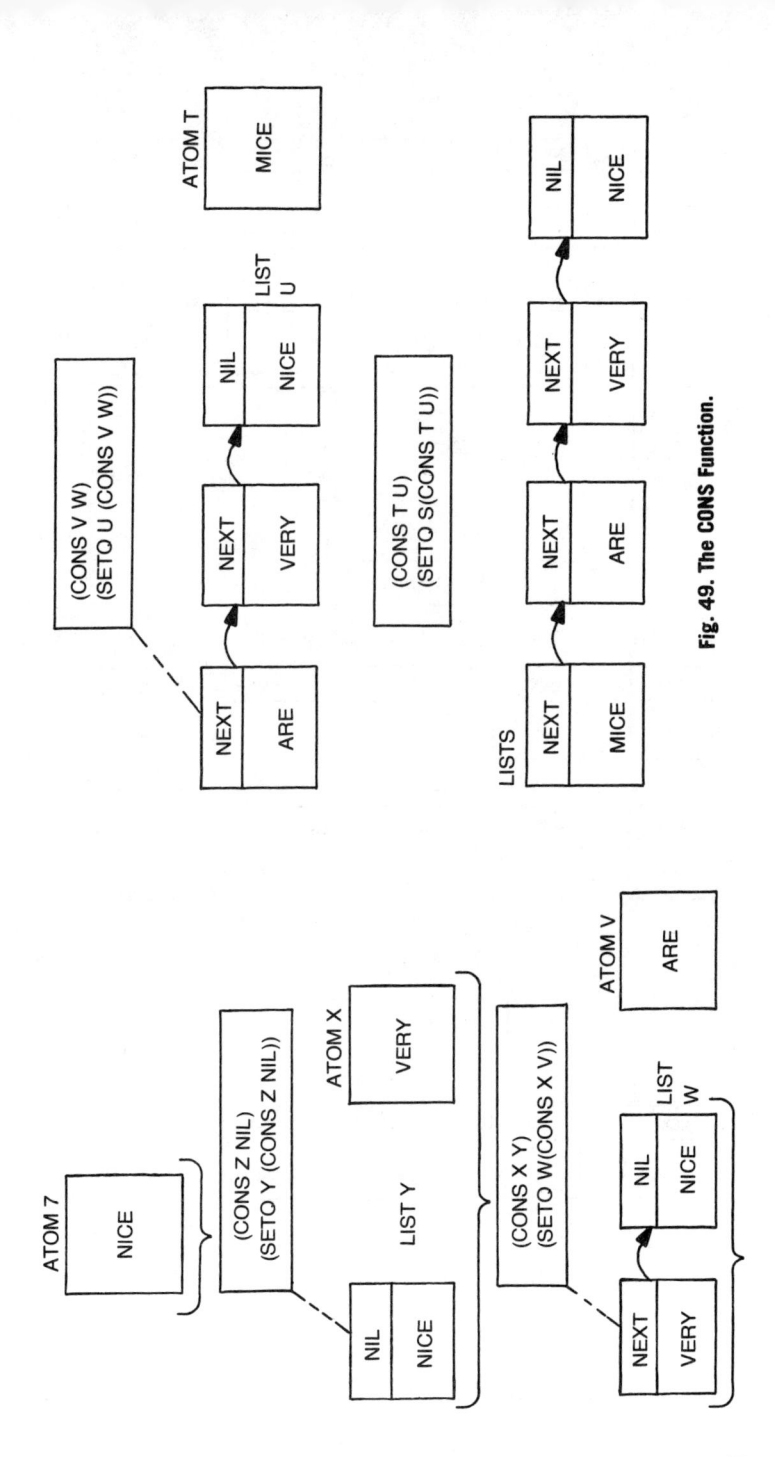

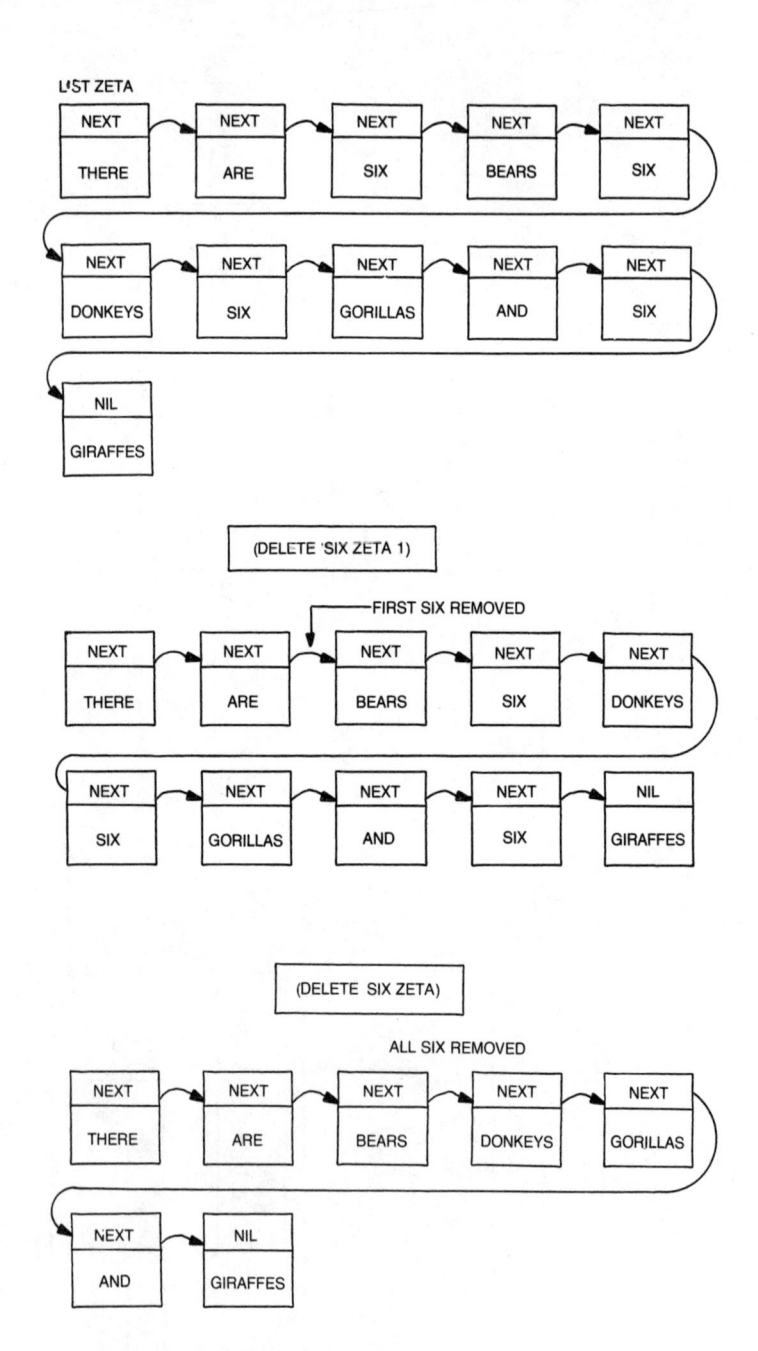

Fig. 50. The DELETE Function.

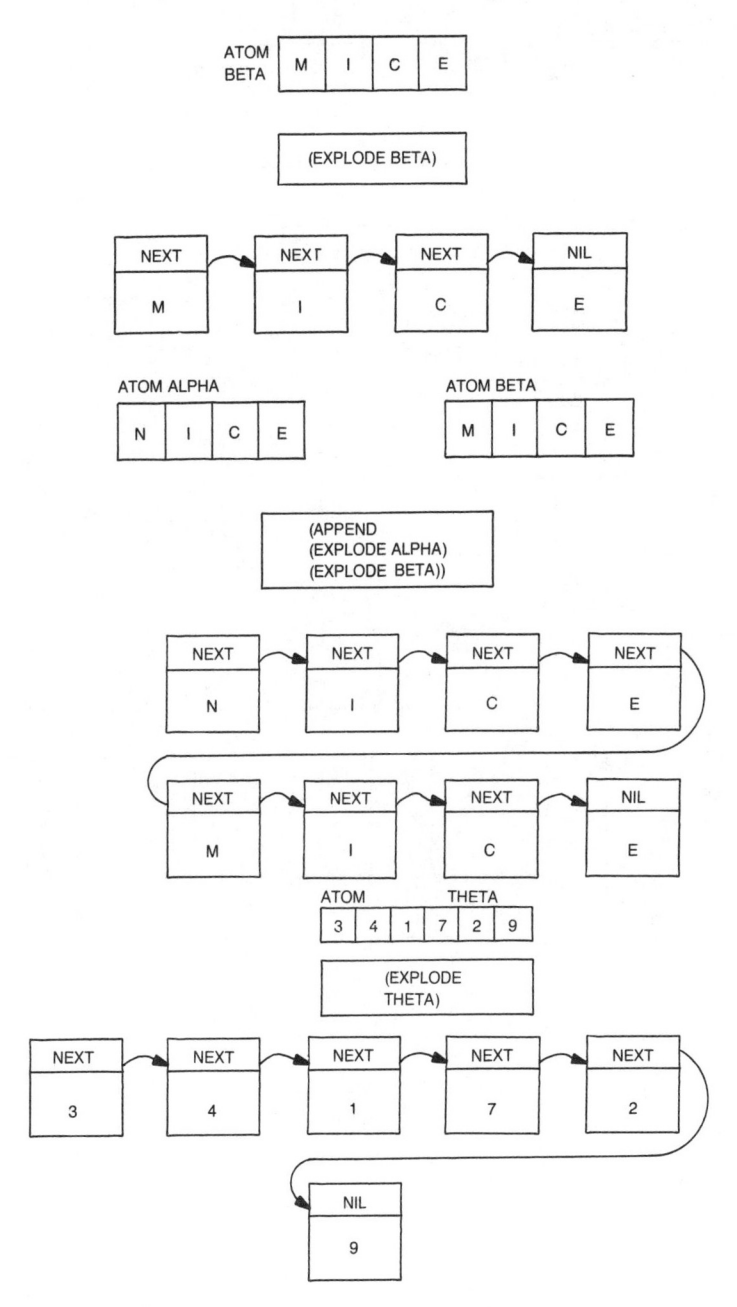

Fig. 51. The EXPLODE Function.

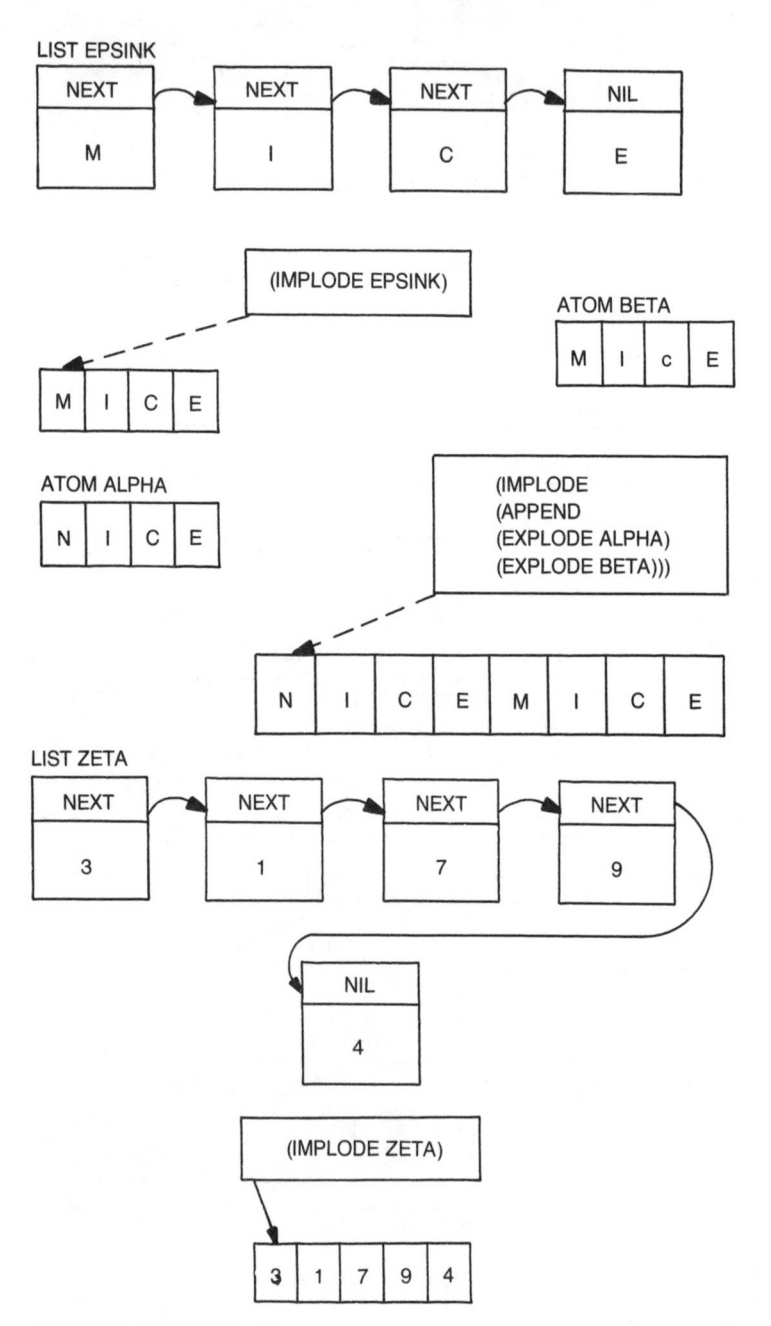

Fig. 52. The IMPLODE Function.

Fig. 53. The LENGTH Function.

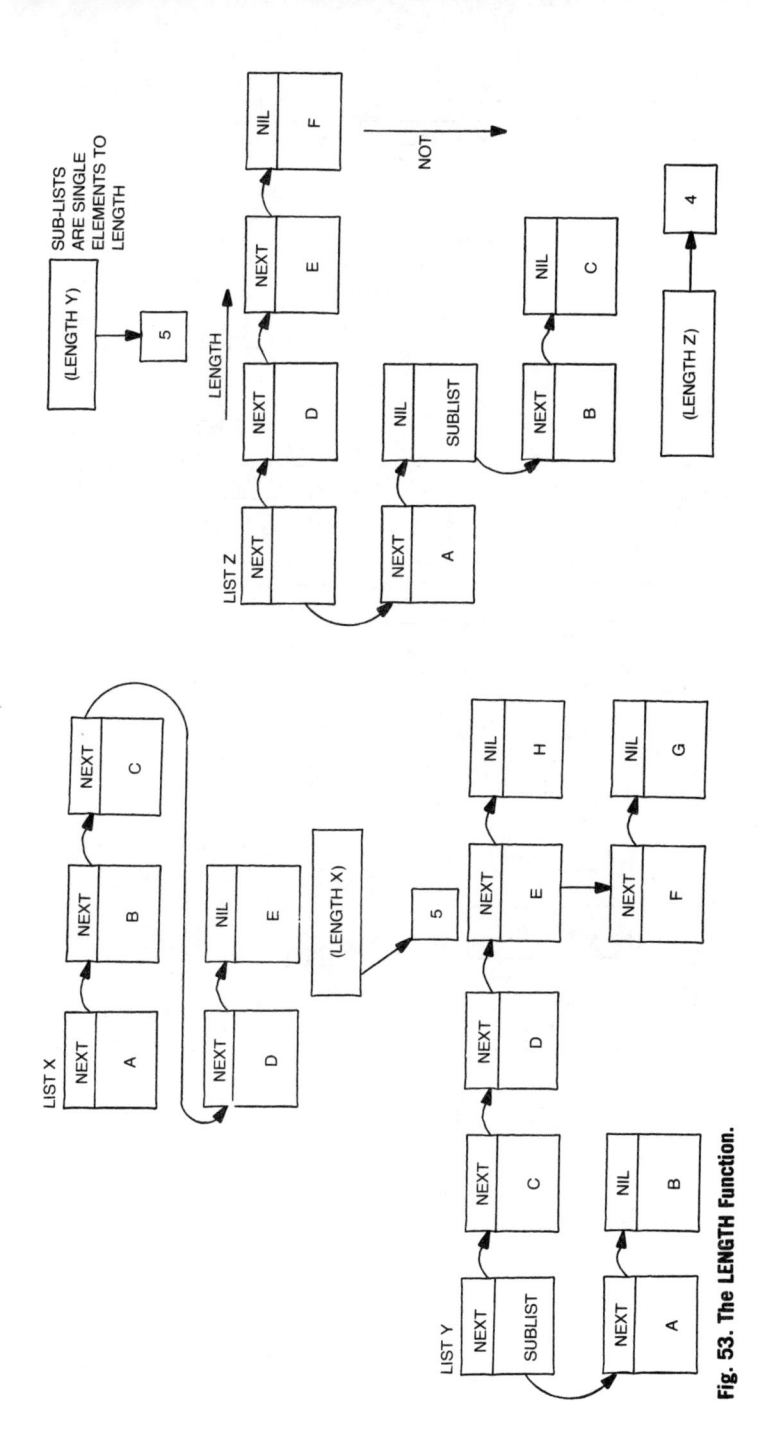

51

THE LIST ALO

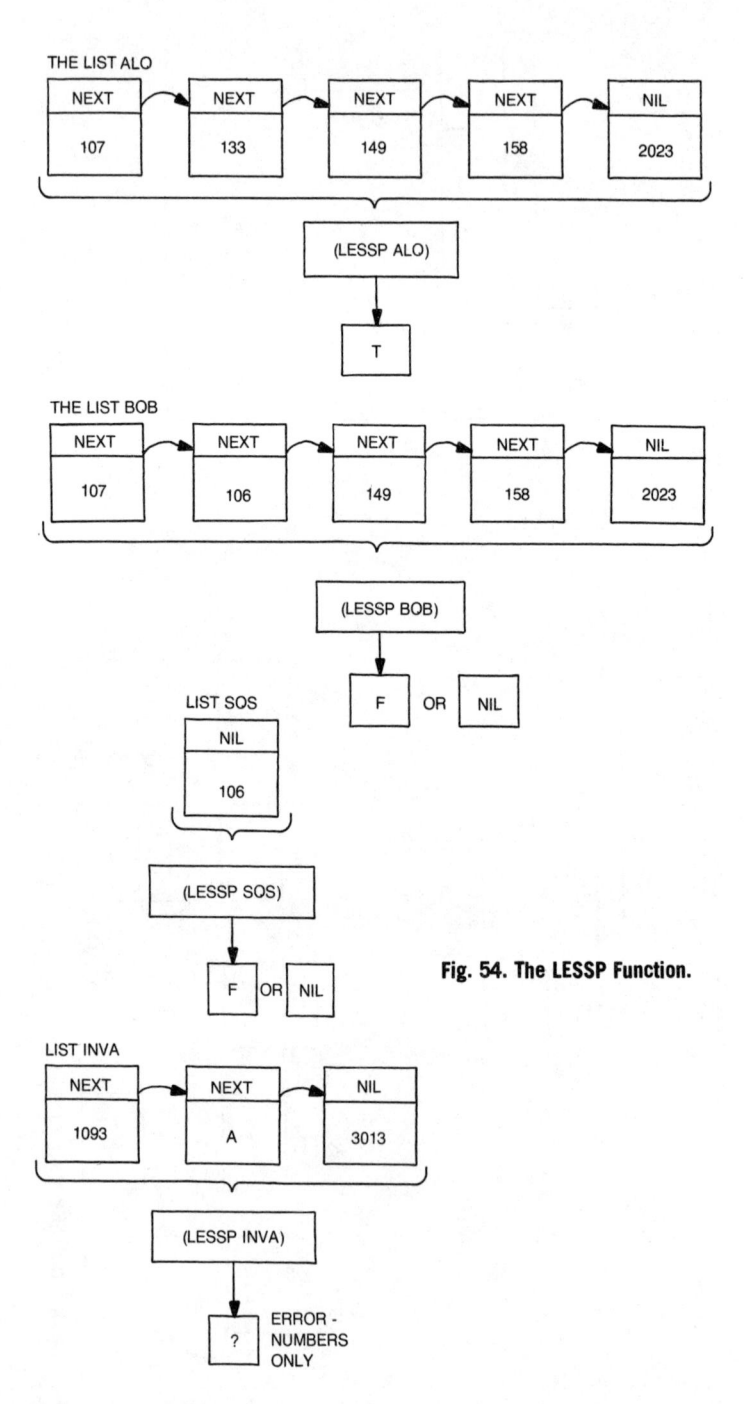

NEXT	NEXT	NEXT	NEXT	NIL
107	133	149	158	2023

(LESSP ALO) → T

THE LIST BOB

NEXT	NEXT	NEXT	NEXT	NIL
107	106	149	158	2023

(LESSP BOB) → F OR NIL

LIST SOS

NIL
106

(LESSP SOS) → F OR NIL

Fig. 54. The LESSP Function.

LIST INVA

NEXT	NEXT	NIL
1093	A	3013

(LESSP INVA) → ? ERROR - NUMBERS ONLY

52

Fig. 55. The LIST Function.

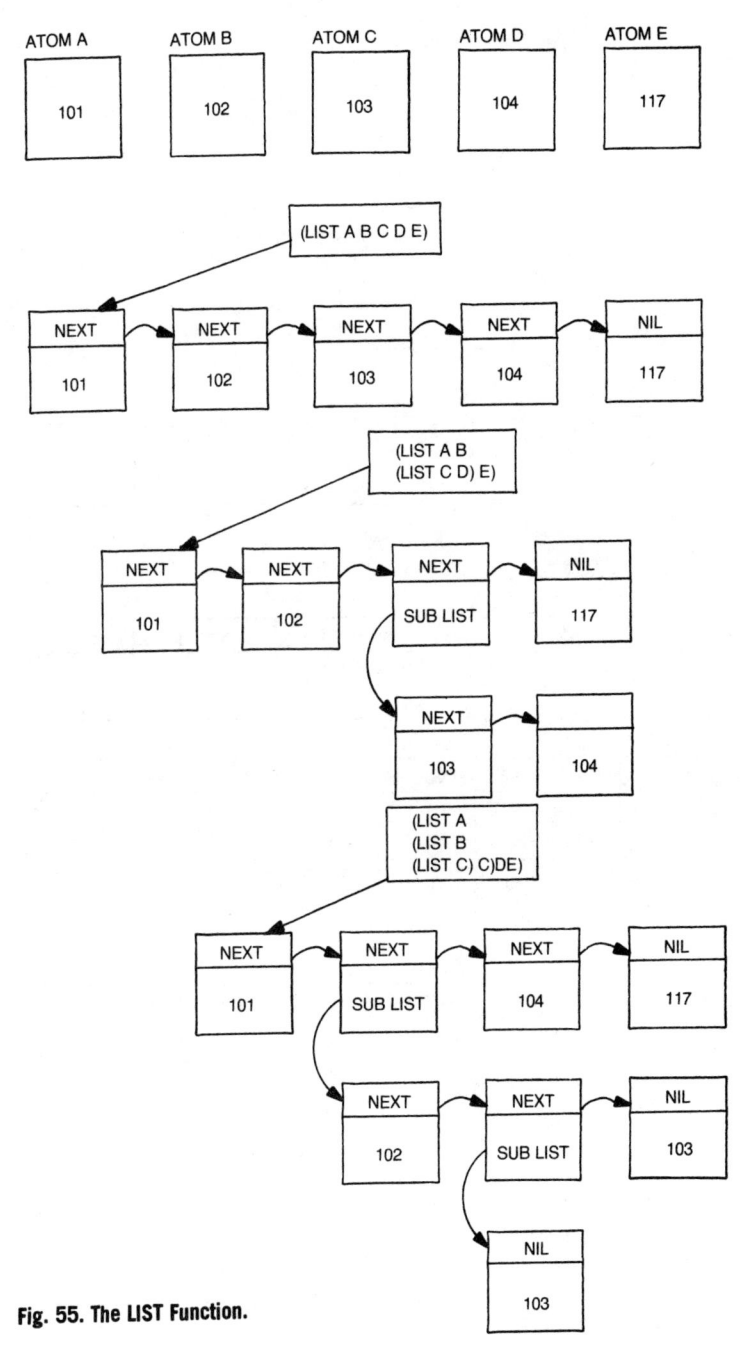

THE DOUBLE FUNCTION

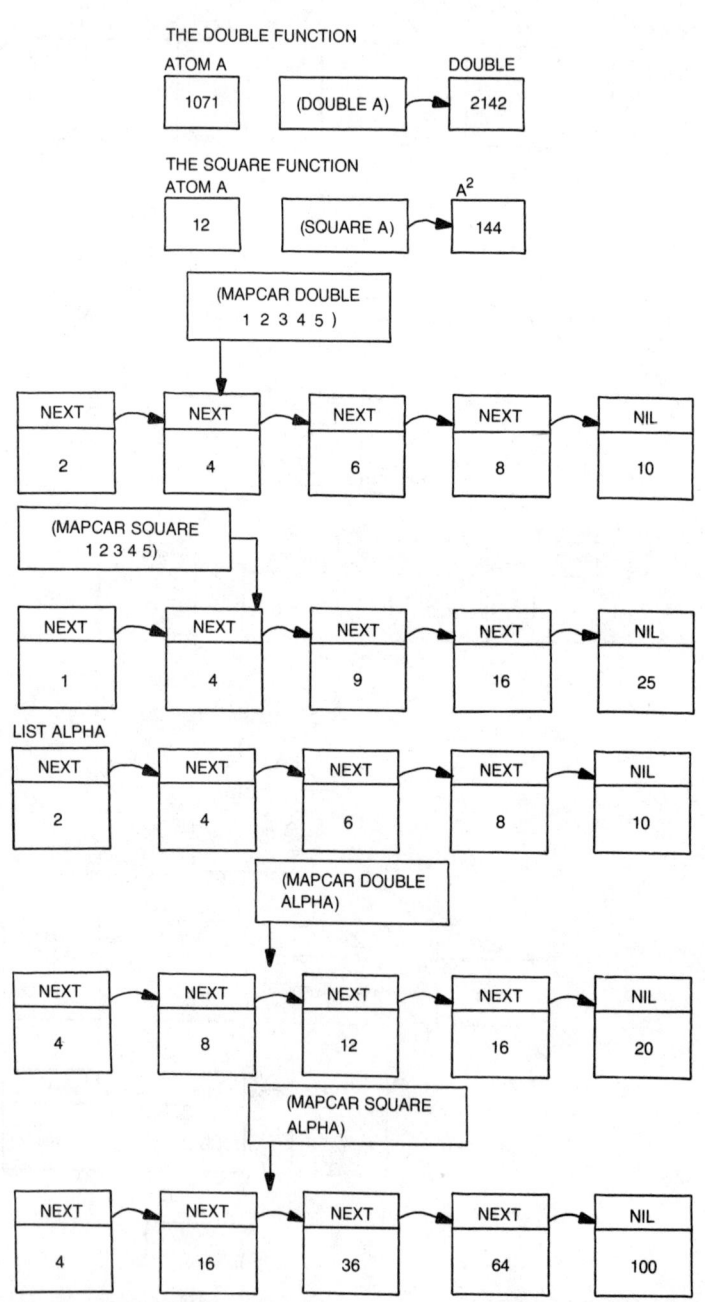

ATOM A   DOUBLE

| 1071 | (DOUBLE A) → | 2142 |

THE SQUARE FUNCTION

ATOM A A^2

| 12 | (SQUARE A) → | 144 |

(MAPCAR DOUBLE 1 2 3 4 5)

| NEXT | NEXT | NEXT | NEXT | NIL |
| 2 | 4 | 6 | 8 | 10 |

(MAPCAR SQUARE 1 2 3 4 5)

| NEXT | NEXT | NEXT | NEXT | NIL |
| 1 | 4 | 9 | 16 | 25 |

LIST ALPHA

| NEXT | NEXT | NEXT | NEXT | NIL |
| 2 | 4 | 6 | 8 | 10 |

(MAPCAR DOUBLE ALPHA)

| NEXT | NEXT | NEXT | NEXT | NIL |
| 4 | 8 | 12 | 16 | 20 |

(MAPCAR SQUARE ALPHA)

| NEXT | NEXT | NEXT | NEXT | NIL |
| 4 | 16 | 36 | 64 | 100 |

Fig. 56. The MAPCAR Function.

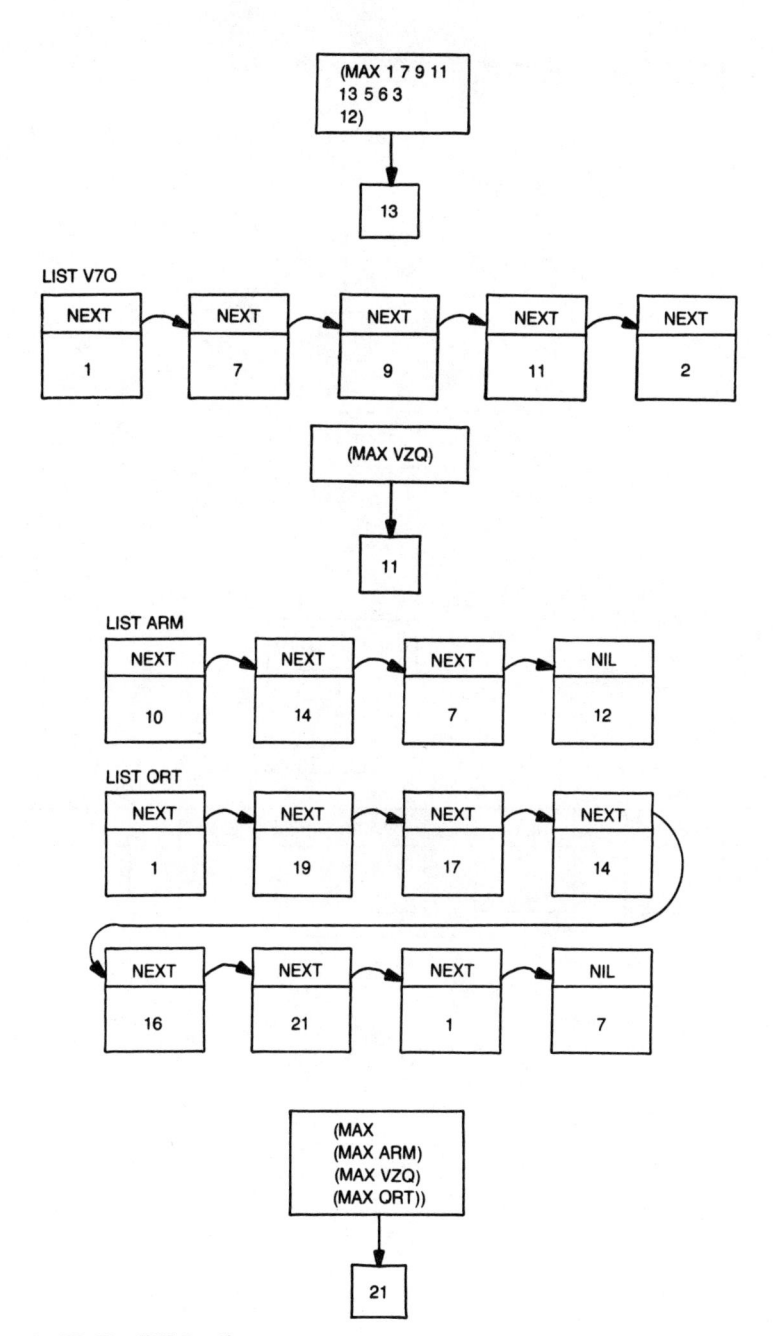

Fig. 57. The MAX Function.

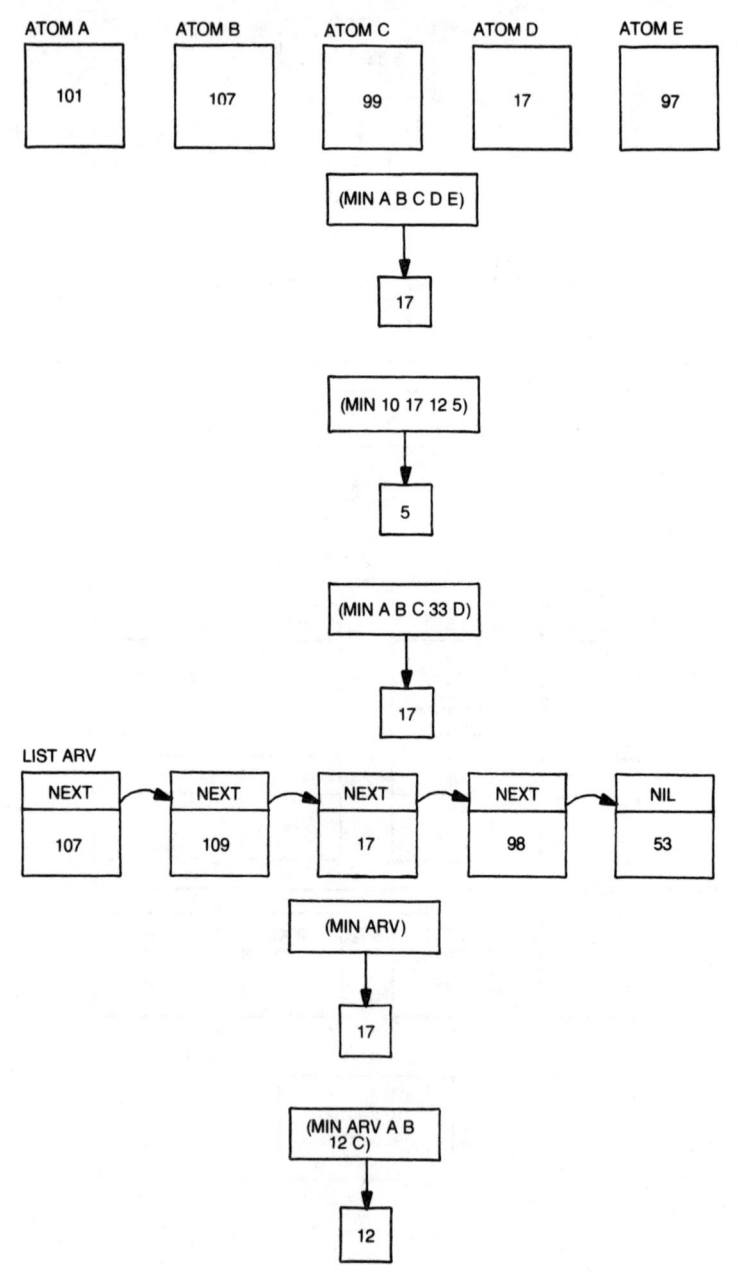

Fig. 58. The MIN Function.

function	definition	example
REVERSE	Reverses the order of the elements in a list.	(REVERSE L) (Fig. 59)
RETURN	Causes the S-expression to be returned as the value of the PROG it appears in.	(RETURN S)
SET	Returns the second argument. The first argument must evaluate to an atom and that atom's value becomes the value of the second argument.	(SET S1 S2)

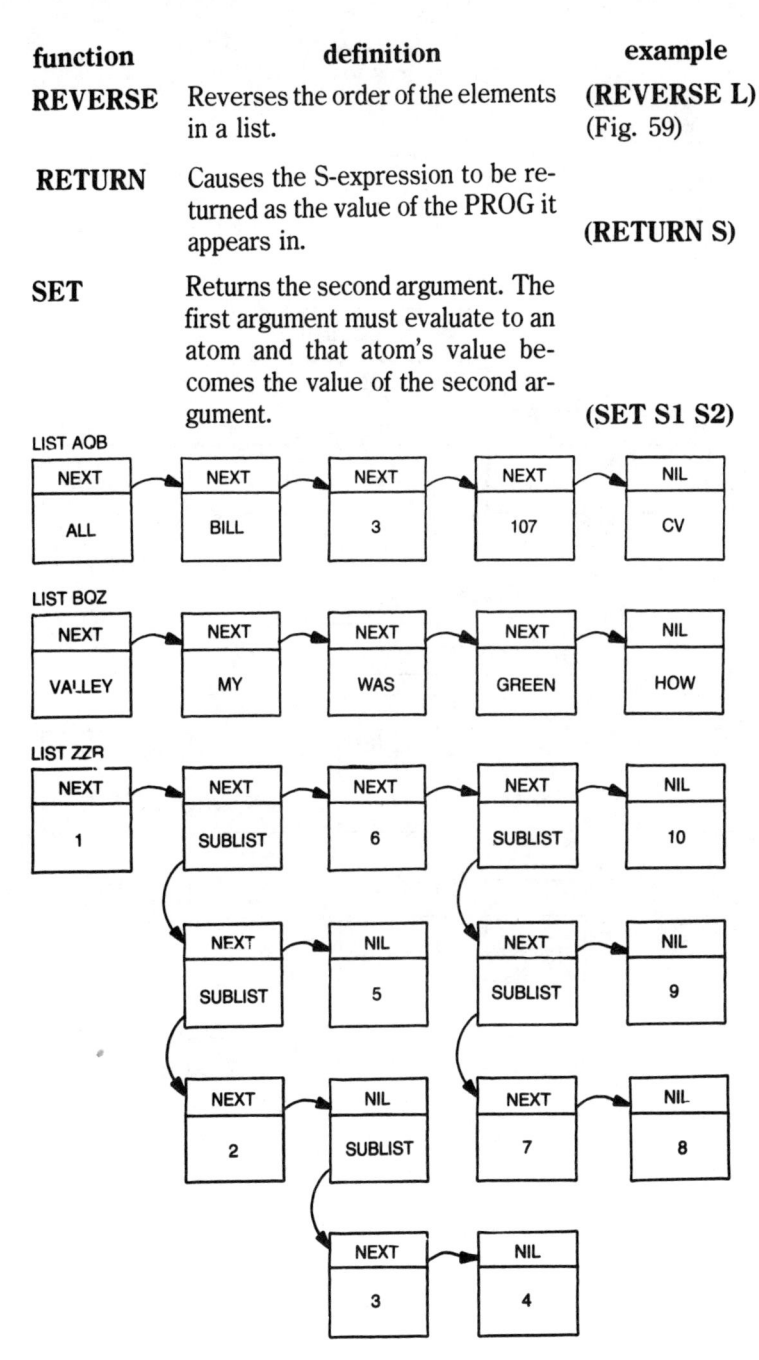

LIST AOB: NEXT/ALL → NEXT/BILL → NEXT/3 → NEXT/107 → NIL/CV

LIST BOZ: NEXT/VALLEY → NEXT/MY → NEXT/WAS → NEXT/GREEN → NIL/HOW

LIST ZZR: NEXT/1 → SUBLIST/NEXT → NEXT/6 → SUBLIST/NEXT → NIL/10

    SUBLIST/NEXT → NIL/5   SUBLIST/NEXT → NIL/9
    SUBLIST/NEXT → NIL/2   NEXT/7 → NIL/8
    SUBLIST/NEXT → NIL
    NEXT/3 → NIL/4

Fig. 59. The REVERSE Function.

(REVERSE AOB)

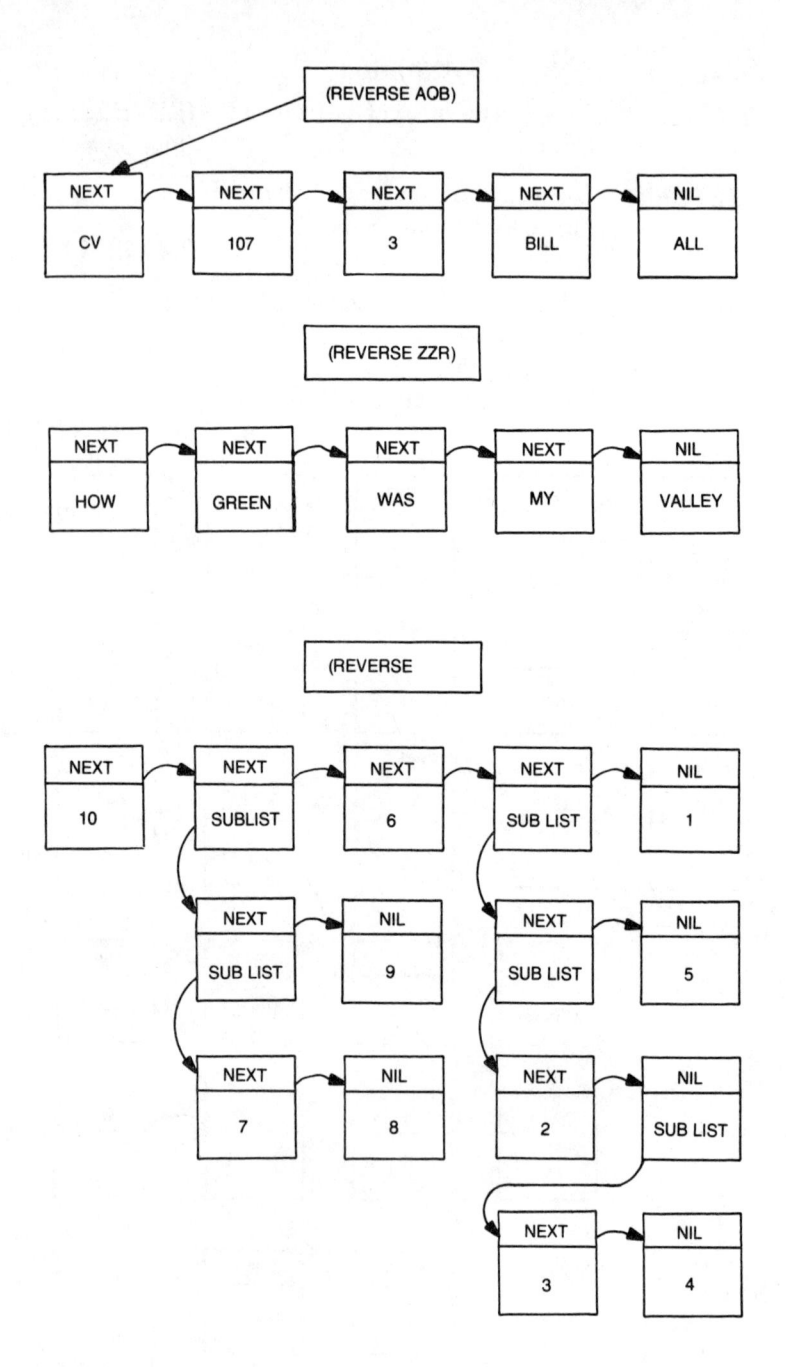

NEXT	NEXT	NEXT	NEXT	NIL
CV	107	3	BILL	ALL

(REVERSE ZZR)

NEXT	NEXT	NEXT	NEXT	NIL
HOW	GREEN	WAS	MY	VALLEY

(REVERSE

NEXT	NEXT	NEXT	NEXT	NIL
10	SUBLIST	6	SUB LIST	1

NEXT	NIL		NEXT	NIL
SUB LIST	9		SUB LIST	5

NEXT	NIL		NEXT	NIL
7	8		2	SUB LIST

NEXT	NIL
3	4

Fig. 59. The REVERSE Function, cont. from page 57.

58

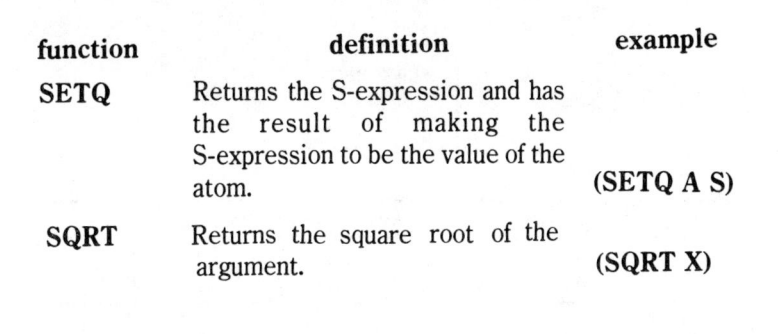

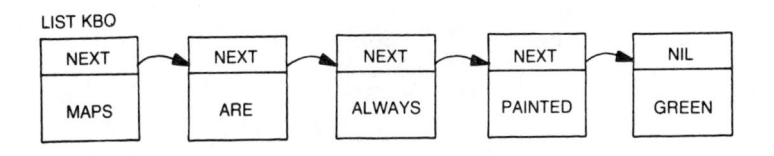

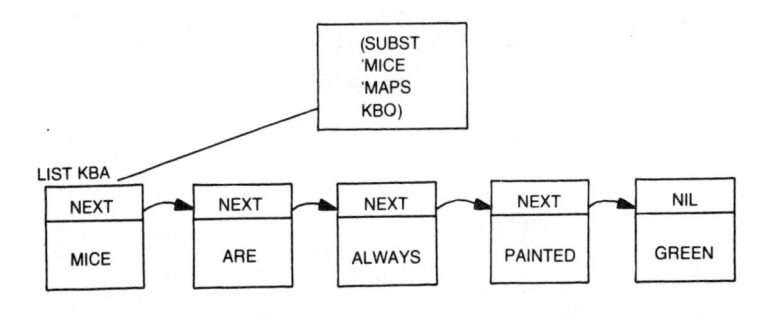

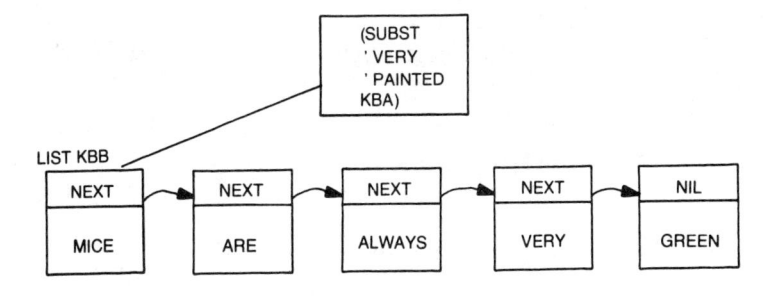

function	definition	example
SETQ	Returns the S-expression and has the result of making the S-expression to be the value of the atom.	(SETQ A S)
SQRT	Returns the square root of the argument.	(SQRT X)

LIST KBO

NEXT → NEXT → NEXT → NEXT → NIL
MAPS   ARE   ALWAYS PAINTED GREEN

(SUBST 'MICE 'MAPS KBO)

LIST KBA

NEXT → NEXT → NEXT → NEXT → NIL
MICE   ARE   ALWAYS PAINTED GREEN

(SUBST 'VERY 'PAINTED KBA)

LIST KBB

NEXT → NEXT → NEXT → NEXT → NIL
MICE   ARE   ALWAYS VERY   GREEN

Fig. 60. The SUBST Function.

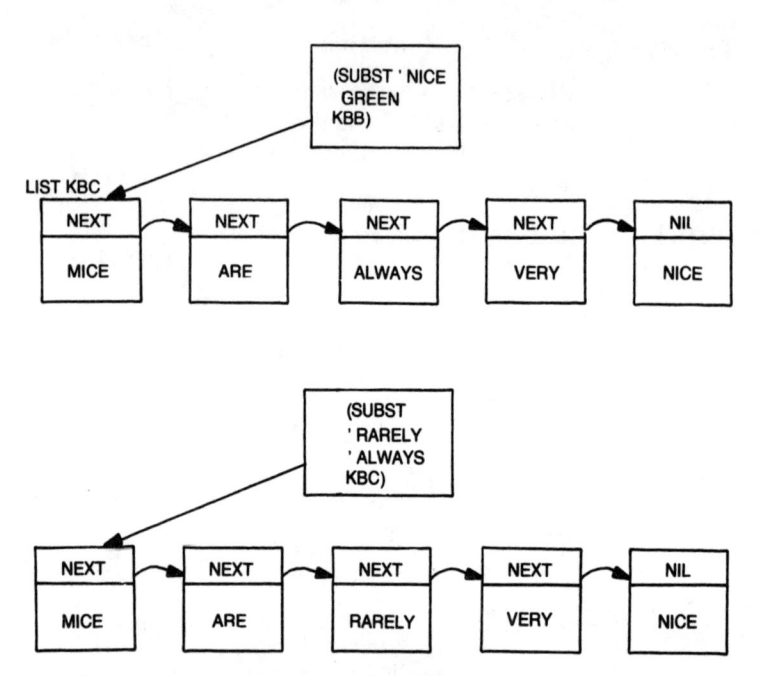

```
       ┌──────────┐
       │(SUBST 'NICE│
       │  GREEN   │
       │  KBB)    │
       └──────────┘
            │
LIST KBC    ▼
┌──────┐  ┌──────┐  ┌──────┐  ┌──────┐  ┌──────┐
│ NEXT │→ │ NEXT │→ │ NEXT │→ │ NEXT │→ │ NIL  │
│ MICE │  │ ARE  │  │ALWAYS│  │ VERY │  │ NICE │
└──────┘  └──────┘  └──────┘  └──────┘  └──────┘


       ┌──────────┐
       │(SUBST    │
       │ 'RARELY  │
       │ 'ALWAYS  │
       │ KBC)     │
       └──────────┘
            │
            ▼
┌──────┐  ┌──────┐  ┌──────┐  ┌──────┐  ┌──────┐
│ NEXT │→ │ NEXT │→ │ NEXT │→ │ NEXT │→ │ NIL  │
│ MICE │  │ ARE  │  │RARELY│  │ VERY │  │ NICE │
└──────┘  └──────┘  └──────┘  └──────┘  └──────┘
```

Fig. 60. The SUBST Function, cont. from page 59

function	definition	example
SUB1	Returns the argument minus one.	**(SUB1 X)**
SUBST	Substitutes S-expression *one* for all occurences of S-expression *two* in the thrid S-expression.	**(SUBST S1 S2 S3)** (Fig. 60)
TERPRI	Causes a carriage return to be exceuted.	**(TERPRI)**
TIMES	Returns the product of all the arguments.	**(TIMES X1...Xn)**
ZEROP	Returns T if the argument is 0.	**(ZEROP X)**

LOGIC

LISP is a functional, symbolic, recursive and list processing language. What else is it?

LISP is also a LOGICAL language.

What does LAMBDA mean when you construct new functions?

LAMBDA defines the argument used by the new function, such as:

(LAMBDA(X Y)(DIFFERENCE(TIMES X Y) (QUOTIENT X Y)))

Which means that the arguments X Y are used in that order and that the function just created is XY-X/Y.

Exactly what are the arguments of LAMBDA?

In general, the first argument of LAMBDA is the list of arguments used by the new function. The second argument of LAMBDA is the S-expression which uses these arguments (Fig. 61).

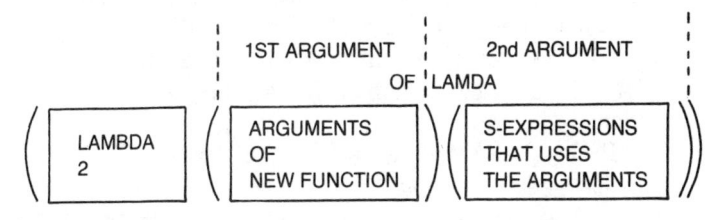

```
( LAMBDA    ( ARGUMENTS      ) ( S-EXPRESSIONS     ) )
    2         OF                 THAT USES
              NEW FUNCTION       THE ARGUMENTS
              ↑                  ↑
              1ST ARGUMENT       2nd ARGUMENT
                    OF LAMDA
```

Fig. 61.

What happens when you call LAMBDA?

The call to LAMBDA is itself a function desciption in terms of value.

How do you enter the LAMBDA constructed function?

Enter it as follows:

(LAMBDA(X Y)(DIFFERENCE(TIMES X Y) (QUOTIENT X Y)))(4 2)

What is the significance of the (4 2) at the end of the LAMBDA expression?

The (4 2) is the list of arguments that the LAMBDA expression is to use in evaluating its constructed function (Fig. 62).

What are the values that LAMBDA can have?

In LISP, LAMBDA can not have a value that is a name, a number of a LIST etc. In this example of LAMBDA (or for that fact any example using the LAMBDA construction), always remember

61

```
                    TO BE USED IN EVALUATION
                 ┌─────────────────┐
                 ▼                 │
( LAMBDA )( ARGUMENTS )( S-EXPRESSION )( 4/2 )
```

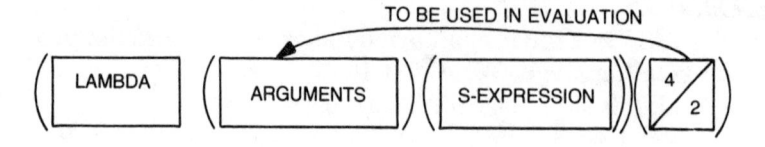

Fig. 62.

that LAMBDA is not truly a function, although it has arguments like functions and it appears first in its list.

Does the history of LAMBDA have any significance on its behavior?

Yes, the LAMBDA construction was first written in 1941 in the book *The Calculi of LAMBDA-Conversion* by Alonzo Church. In his notation, the use of LAMBDA, as in our example is λ x (xy-x/y). LISP must necessarily be precise in wording. For one thing, xy would be a separate ATOM and not the pair of ATOM x and y. (Note: typically upper case is used in LISP. I have used lower-case only to explain Church's formula construction.

How do you define a function with a name?

First write a simple definition with a name, then comes the explanation:

DEFINE (((K(LAMBDA(S)(PLUS S S)))))

This has been written at the TOP level. Use level (see the LISP system). If you want to write this example at an inner level (such as used in a LISP program) you would write:

(DEFINE((QUOTE(K(LAMBDA(S)(PLUS S)))))). This procedure, either case, defines a single function given by a list of two elements. The first of these elements is K, the function name. The second is the function description. This description specifies that the given function has "one" argument. Only the ATOM S is given in the list which is the first argument of LAMBDA. This means, that whenever you call the function K in the future it will require only one argument.

How would you call the function just constructed in the preceeding paragraph?

Since K is now a valid instruction (function), call it in the same manner that you would call any other function. An example would be ("function name" "argument"). In this case you would write (K 2) if you wanted to evaluate the function with an argument of 2.

Can the new function be used like any other function?

Yes, you can use it exactly as if it had been a standard function that resides always in LISP. You can even construct other new functions using the new function—in this case the function K.

What are "formal" and "actual" parameters?
If you write in FORTRAN:
FUNCTION F(A, B, C), then A, B, C are the formal parameters. If you use the function in an expression such as:
SDF(U/H, EZ)
Then U/H, E-R and Z are the actual parameters. The actual parameters can sometimes be expressions, the formal parameters are *never* more complex than single identifiers. But, the formal parameters can stand for arrays or functions as well as variables. There is obviously a correspondence between formal and actual parameters. In the "actual expression," using the FUNCTION created the actual parameters are on a one-to-one correspondence with the formal parameters. Whatever the FUNCTION specifies to do with the first formal parameter in the list is done to the first actual parameter in the expression. Whatever is specified for the second formal parameter in the FUNCTION definition is to be done to the second actual parameter in the expression—and so forth (Fig. 63).

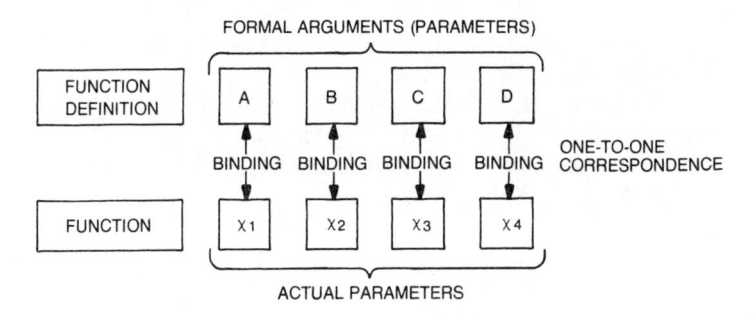

Fig. 63.

What is "BINDING"?
The idea of one-to-one correspondence between formal and actual parameters is called "binding" in mathematical logic.
How does this apply to LISP?
In LISP, the same sort of activity occurs between formal and actual parameters. If you look again at the S-expression given in the paragraph on LAMBDA construction in the section on Logic,

X IS BOUND TO 4

[X ↔ 4]

Y IS BOUND TO 2

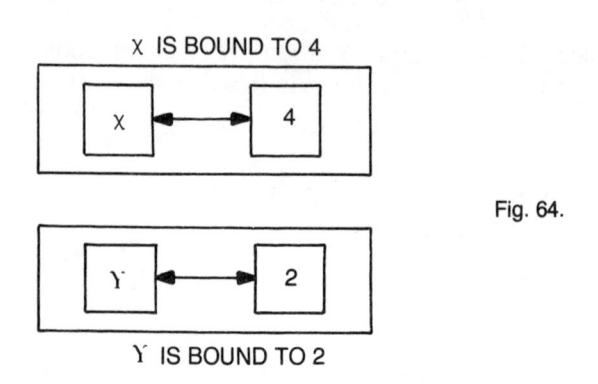

[Y ↔ 2]

Fig. 64.

you can see that X and Y are the formal parameters and 4 and 2 are the actual parameters. X is bound to 4 and Y is bound to 2 (Fig. 64).

Does this imply that every variable in the second argument of a LAMBDA expression is a formal parameter as well?

In the example given, the variables occurring in the second argument were indeed formal parameters. Note that I mean bound variable when I use the word parameter. In LISP, you can also have "free" variables in the second argument or definition expression. A free variable uses as its value its current or present value at the time of execution of the expression containing the free variable. It is not bound to values that are given with the expression.

How can you compare binding a variable and performing an assignment?

Binding a variable and assigning a value to a variable are operations that LISP internally treats almost the same (Fig. 65). For example, whenever you perform a SETQ or SET operation you are, in effect, binding variables.

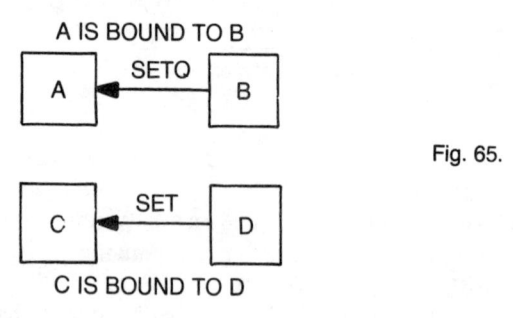

A IS BOUND TO B

[A ←SETQ— B]

[C ←SET— D]

C IS BOUND TO D

Fig. 65.

If this is the case, you can call the SETQ and and SET operations binding operations?

64

Yes, and later I will refer to a function call using SETQ or SET as binding a variable (Fig. 66). For example:
(SETQ X 6)
You are binding the variable X to 6, you can also write:
(SET(QUOTE A)(QUOTE (4 7 9)))
and say that you are binding A to the value (4 7 9).

Fig. 66.

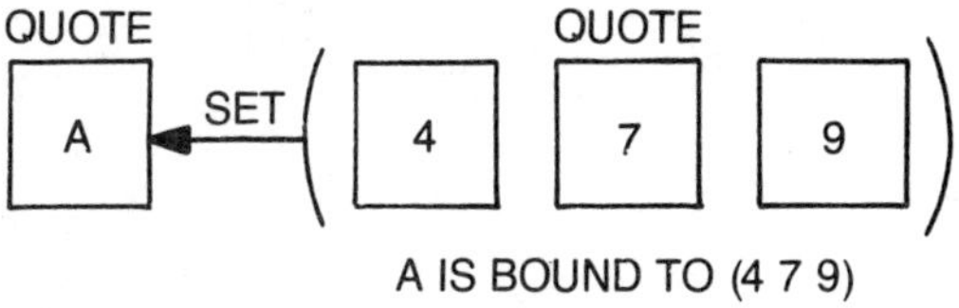

```
QUOTE          QUOTE
[ A ] ←SET ( [ 4 ] [ 7 ] [ 9 ] )
```

A IS BOUND TO (4 7 9)

LIST PROCESSING

In which ways can you use LISP now?
You can make calls to system functions (functions that are standard or already defined in LISP) and you can define simple functions.

In order to define more complex functions, what do you need?
You need to use the LISP LIST processing functions.

What are these LIST processing functions?
For the time being, I will cover only the more primitive functions, such as "CAR," "DCR" and "CONS." Before going any further it should be pointed out that all functions in LISP are said as words and never spelled out. Therefore, the function CDR is pronounced "couder," and never spoken as the C D R function.

Why are CAR CDR and CONS called primitive LIST functions?
Because all other list functions are based on these three functions.

What does the CAR function do?
The CAR function takes as its argument a LIST and returns as its value the first element of the list (Fig. 67). The list must have a name, usually a single letter, and you can refer to that list by using its name. Consider the following LISTS:
  if A is (3 4 5)
  if B is (5(3(6(4))))
  if C is ((4 6) (84))
  if D is ((((5)9)5)3)

65

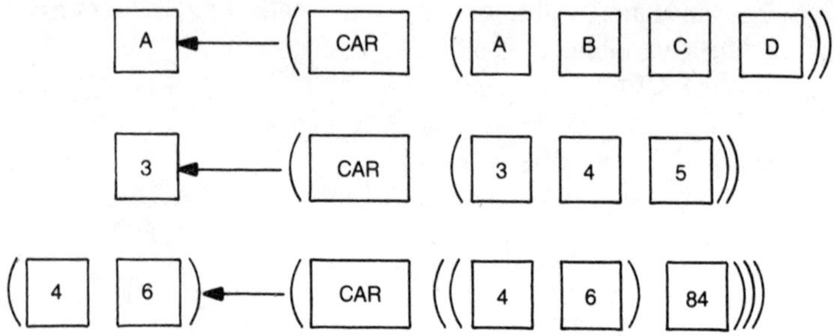

Fig. 67.

Then
(CAR A) is 3
(CAR B) is 5
(CAR C) is (4 6)
(CAR D) is (((5)9)5)

What is the CDR function?

The CDR function takes as its argument (like the CAR function) a LIST (Fig. 68). Its value is the remainder of the list with the first element removed. Try CDR on the following LISTS:
if A is (8 8 7 6)
if B is (3(7(9(3))))
if C is ((4 5)(9 7))
if D is ((((5)6)2)9)

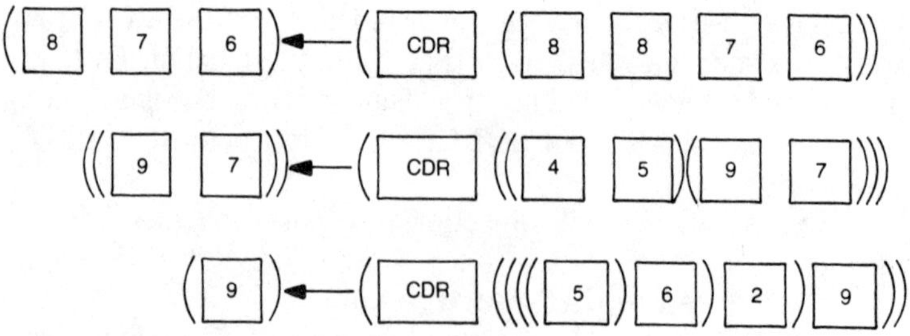

Fig. 68.

Then
(CDR A) is (8 7 6)
(CDR B) is ((7(9(3))))
(CDR C) is ((9 7))
(CDR D) is (9)

When does (CAR A) make no sense?
If A stands for an ATOM, (CAR A) has no meaning and in fact will cause a LISP system error.
When does (CDR A) make no sense?
If A stands for a list containing exactly one element, (CDR A) makes no sense if you consider the definition of CDR given earlier. However, in the case (CDR A) of the list A containing only one element, (CDR A) returns the special ATOM NIL. Which, if you recall, also means False. Here again you have another function for the ATOM NIL (Fig. 69).

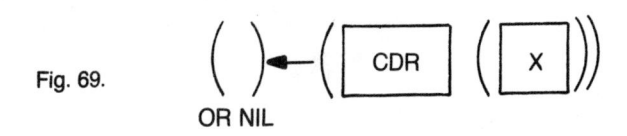

Fig. 69. ( ) ← ([CDR] ([X]))
OR NIL

You know what CAR and CDR do. What about CONS?
CONS is the function that puts back together what CAR and CDR have taken apart.
How does CONS operate in LISP?
CONS has as its value a list. Its arguments (it requires two) are the results of CAR and CDR operations, respectively, applied to that list (Fig. 70). Consider some examples:
If A is 5 and B is (6 7 9)
if C is 9 and D is ((3(5(8))))
if E is (3 4) and F is ((3 5))
if G is (((5)8)3) and H is (3)
then
(CONS A B) is (5 6 7 9)
(CONS C D) is (9(3(5(8))))
(CONS E F) is ((3 4)(3 5))
(CONS G H) is (((5)8)3)3)

The results produced by CONS, applied to any two arguments, is as follows. The second argument should be a list. To get the value of CONS, append one more element on to the front of this list. This would be the first argument of CONS which can be anything, including an ATOM.
Are the definitions of CAR, CDR and CONS complete?
No, but I will discuss them again in respect to definition later.
What is the second element of any list?
The first element of the CDR of that list is for example:
(6 7 8)

67

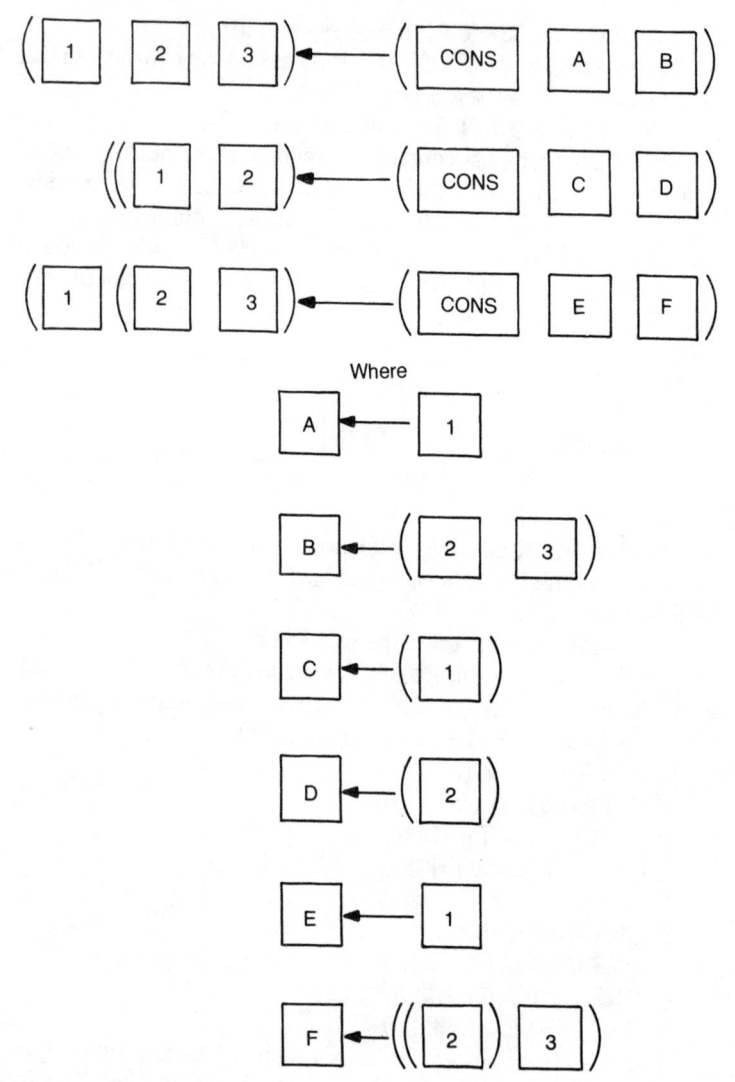

Fig. 70.

Obviously, the second element is 7 and the value of the CDR operation on this list is (7 8). The 7 is the first element of the value returned.

In general, if you want to isolate the second element, what would you do?

You would combine operations of CAR and CDR. Assume you have a list named K and that the list was:

68

(4 5 6 7)

If you write:

(CAR(CDR K))

you would have as a value the element 5. The operation is straight forward. The (CDR K) has as its value (5 6 7) which are the elements remaining after the first element is removed. If you apply the CAR function to the new list (5 6 7) you get the value 5. Use the list functions in the same manner as the arithmetic functions. Therefore, you can see that the inner S-expression (CDR K) is evaluated first. Then the CAR function uses as its argument the value produced by the first operation, CDR (Fig. 71).

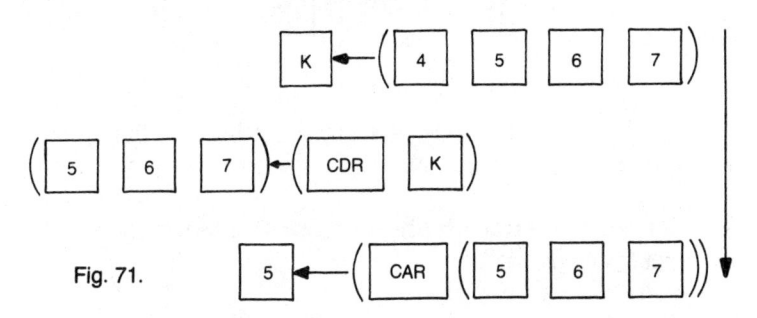

Fig. 71.

Can you write (CAR(CDR L)) where L is any list in another manner?

Yes, you can write (CADR L), which is exactly the same as: CAR(CDRL))

(experiment a little with (CAR(CDR L)). Use the following lists:

(2 3 4)

(5 6) (7 8)(7 6))

(5 9 3 7 6)

Assuming each list has the same name S, use the (CAR(CDR S)) function on them. You can also use the composite function (CADR S).

(CADR S) is 3, when S is (2 3 4)

(CADR S) is (7 8), when S is ((5 6)(7 8)(7 6))

(CADR S) is 9, when S is (5 9 3 7 6)

Can you extract the third element as easily?

Yes, you can write:

(CADR(CDR L))

or

(CAR(CDR(CDR L)))

```
         K ◄── ( 1  2  3  4 )

( 2  3  4 ) ◄── ( CDR  K )

  ( 3  4 ) ◄── ( CDR ( 2  3  4 ))

      3 ◄── ( CAR ( 3  4 ))
```

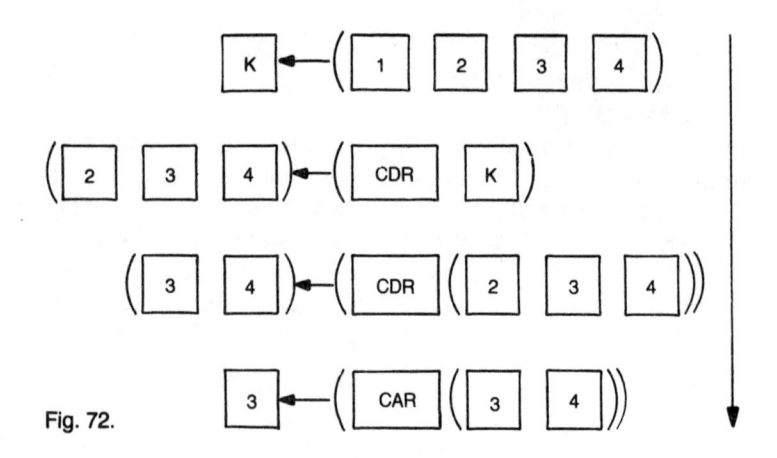

Fig. 72.

In either case, the third element of the list L is the second element of (CDR L) (Fig. 72).

Can this function also be written in an easier fashion?
Yes, you can write:
(CAR(CDR(CDR L)))
as
(CADDR L)
Where (CADDR L) has exactly the same meaning as (CAR(CDR(CDR L))) or
(CADR(CDR L)).

Is there some general rule to follow when constructing these easier to write functions?
Yes, generally in LISP, the user is allowed to create special functions for selecting elements by using the following rule. The function name must start with a C. It is the followed by any reasonable amount of A's and D's—usually around five. Each A stands for the function CAR, while each D stands for the function CDR. Also, the function created must end in an R. Therefore, you can create many different functions. The A,s and D's are taken in order from left to right in the composite function.

Does LISP have any type of concatenation function?
Yes, it is called APPEND (Fig. 73). Concatenate some examples:

If A is (3 4 5) and B is (6 7)
if C is (4 5 6 7 8) and D is (1 2 3)
if E is (1 1 1) and F is (2 2 2)

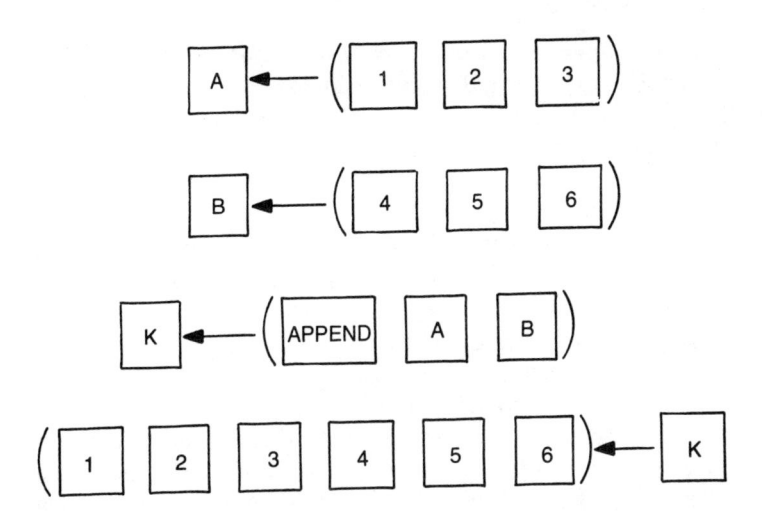

Fig. 73.

Then
(APPEND A B) is (3 4 5 6 7)
(APPEND C D) is (4 5 6 7 8 1 2 3)
(APPEND E F) is (1 1 1 2 2 2)
Also note that if you wrote:
(CONS E F)
you would have:
(CONS E F) is ((1 1 1)2 2 2)

PREDICATES

A sentence in English has what parts?

If it is a regular declarative sentence, it has a subject and a predicate (Fig. 74).

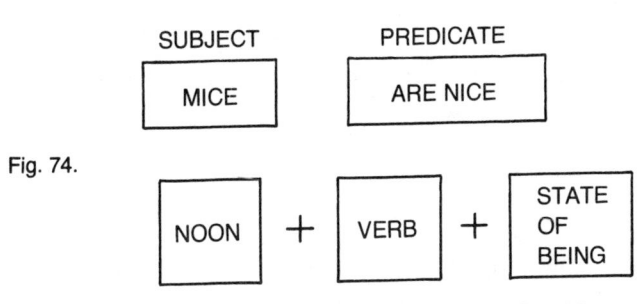

Fig. 74.

ALL STATEMENTS ARE PREDICATES

What does this have to do with LISP?
Predicates can be either true or false. Look at some examples of sentences in English first. LISP is a computer language. An ATOM is two S-expressions added together. The CAR function returns the first element of a list. The CDR function returns the last element in a list.

In the first statement, LISP is the subject and *is a computer language* is the predicate. The statement is "true." In the second statement ATOM is the subject and the statement is "false." CAR is the subject of the third statement and it is "TRUE." CDR is the subject of the fourth statement and it is "false."

Why is this important?
Predicates are common in computer programming languages—even if they are not called predicates. The operations EQ and NE in FORTRAN are predicates since they tell something about the subject and they stand for equal and not equal respectively. LISP has predicates and they too can be either true of false.

Is this what T and F are about?
Yes, if a statement (predicate) is true the value of the predicate is T (true). If it is false it has the value NIL. Remember, the symbol NIL is usually used for false and not F.

Is a predicate a function?
Yes, every construction in LISP is a function!

What does the function ATOM do?
The function ATOM has as its arguments either ATOMS or LISTS. If the argument is an ATOM, the value is T (true). If the argument is a list, the value is NIL (false). You can say that the function ATOM is asking the question "is my argument an ATOM?"

How do you use the function ATOM?
Write some statements and see. Use a name or symbol to represent the list or ATOM:
if A is 7
if B is A (the symbol, do not be concerned with the value)
if C is (4 8 2)
then
(ATOM A) is T
(ATOM B) is T
(ATOM C) is NIL

This is because A is indeed an ATOM and B is also true because it is an ATOM while C is false because (4 8 2) is a list.

What does the function NULL do?

The function NULL, tests whether or not its argument is NIL or not. If its argument is NIL the value of NULL is NIL.

What is the significance of T in the previous question?

It stands for anything else that is not NIL, such as a list or an ATOM. T is not a LISP construction, but merely stands for anything that is true or not NIL.

What are some examples of the NULL function?

use the following examples:
if A is 7
if B is A (the symbol)
if C is (4 8 2)
if D is NIL
then
(NULL A) is NIL
(NULL B) is NIL
(NULL C) is NIL
(NULL D) is T

obviously, the arguments 7, A, (4 8 2) are not NIL. Therefore, NULL function returns a NIL, but the last argument is indeed NIL and therefore you have the value of NULL as being T.

What value would NULL have in this example (and X is a single element):

(NULL(CDR X))?

See the section "when does (CDR A) make no sense?" under LISP'S list processing. The value of NULL would be T, because CDR returns a NIL everytime it has an argument that is a single element.

What is the EQUAL function and what does it do?

The EQUAL function test to see if its two arguments are EQUAL, or to be precise, "identical." Try a few examples:
If A is (4 5 6) and B is (4 5 6)
if C is 9 and D is 19
if E is (TIMES 5 4) and F is 20
if G is (TIMES 5 4) and H is (TIMES 5 4)
if I is ((3 4) 7) and J is (3(4 7))
then
(EQUAL A B) is T
(EQUAL C D) is NIL
(EQUAL E F) is NIL
(EQUAL G H) is T
(EQUAL I J) is NIL

As you can see, it is not enough for the values of the arguments to be equal such as in the case of E and F. To be true or T the arguments must be identical. There is also an EQ function that operates on ATOMS only.

What is the ZEROP function?

The ZEROP function tests to see if its argument is zero. The letter P in ZEROP stands for predicate. If the argument is ZERO, then the value of ZEROP is T. Otherwise it is NIL. Try some examples:

if A is 987
if B is 56
if C is 0
if D is 28
Then
(ZEROP A) is NIL
(ZEROP B) is NIL
(ZEROP C) is T
(ZEROP D) is NIL

What does the function GREATERP do?

The GREATERP function tests to determine whether or not its first argument (it requires two) is greater than its second argument. The following are some examples:

if A is 5 and B is 7
if C is 45 and D is 44
if E is 34 and F is 81
if G is 50 and H is 50
Then
(GREATERP A B) is NIL
(GREATERP C D) is T
(GREATERP E F) is NIL
(GREATERP G H) is NIL

SECOND REVIEW

What is the (CAR A), where A is (A B C)?
A, because it is the first element of the non-null list.
What is the (CAR A), where A is ((S D F) H J K)?
((S D)), because it is the first S-expression.
What is the (CAR A), where A is CHEESE?
No answer, you can not ask the CAR of an ATOM
What is the (CAR A), where A is ()?
No answer, you can not ask the CAR of a null list.
The CAR function is defined for what?

The CAR function is defined only for non-null lists.

What is the (CAR A), where A is ((MICE) (ARE) (NICE))?
((MICE))

What is the (CAR A), where A is (MICE ARE NICE)?
((MICE))

What is the (CDR B), where B is (6 8 9)?
(8 9)

What is the (CDR B), where B is ((S D F) J K L)?
(J K L)

What is the (CDR B), where B is (MICE ARE NICE)?
(ARE NICE)

What is the (CDR B), where B is ((MICE)(ARE)(NICE))?
((ARE)(NICE

What is the (DR B), where B is (MICE)?
NIL

What is the (CDR B), where B is MICE?
No answer, you can not ask the CDR of an ATOM.

What is the (CDR B), where B is ()?
No answer, you can not ask the CDR of a null list.

The CDR function is defined for what?
The CDR function is defined for non-null lists only.

What is the (CAR(CDR A)) of (where A is): Y((D)(T Y) (C))?
((T Y))

What is the (CDR(CDR A), where A is: ((D) (T Y) (C))?
((C))

What is the CONS of the ATOM MICE and the list: (ARE NICE)?
(MICE ARE NICE)

What is the (CONS A B), where A is (MICE) and B is (ARE NICE)?
((MICE) ARE NICE)

What are the arguments of the CONS function?
The arguments are any S-expression (ATOM or LIST) for the first and any LIST for the second argument.

What is (CONS A B), where A is K and B is ( )?
(K)

What is the (CONS A B), where A is MICE and B is ARE NICE?
No answer, the second argument must be a list.

75

What is (CONS A B), where A is (MICE) and B is ARE NICE?

No answer, the second argument regardless of the first must be a LIST.

What is (CONS A(CAR B)), where A is F and B is (C D)?

No answer, because the CAR function returned an ATOM and the second argument of CONS must be a list.

What is the (CONS A(CAR B)), where A is F and B is ((C)D)?

(F C)

What is the CONS A(CDR B)), where A is D and B is (B C D)?

(D C D)

HOW PREDICATES ARE USED

What is the difference between conditional statements in FORTRAN and BASIC or in LISP?

A conditional statement in BASIC or in FORTRAN consists of if statements, while in LISP conditional statements are composed of functions. Remember, all constructions in LISP are always composed of functions. LISP is a functional language.

What is the name of the function that allows conditional tests?

It is called COND.

For example, how would you interpret the following expression: (COND((ZEROP A)(SETQ K 19)))?

Read the above expression in the question to mean. If A is zero then set K to the value 19 (Fig. 75).

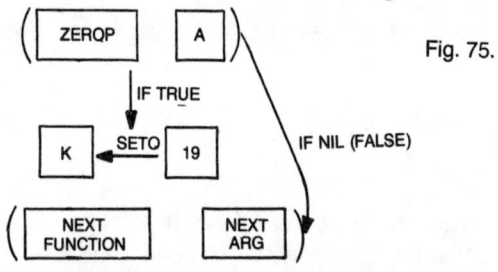

Fig. 75.

How does COND operate?

The function called COND has an indefinite number of arguments. Each and every argument must be a pair or a list of two elements. The first element in the pair is the condition, the second element is either an action to perform or a quantity (Fig. 76).

What does the following expression mean:
(COND((ZEROP A)9)((GREATERP A C)8)(T O))?

76

Fig. 76.

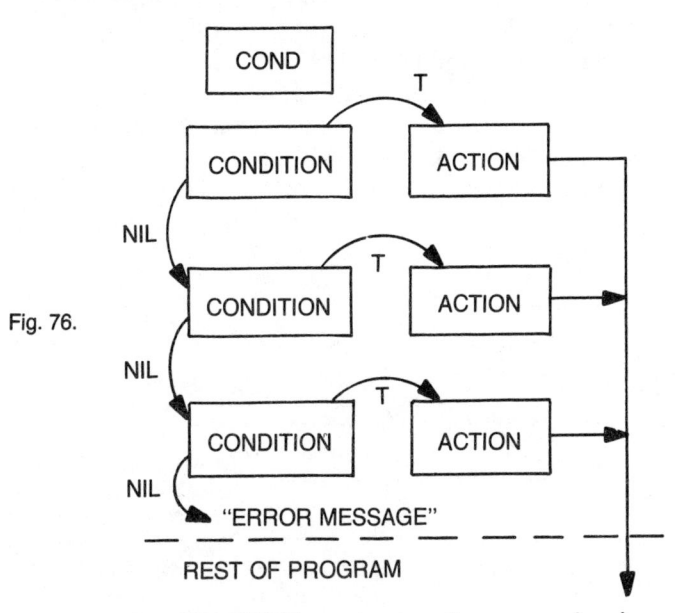

The first function COND states that the expression is a conditional.

The first pair is:

((ZEROP A)9)

If A is 0, then the expression has a value of 9. The COND function looks at every pair, one by one, going from left to right. It continues to look at pairs until a test is true or satisfied. The COND function does not check whether a condition is true, but rather if it is NIL, If the condition is to be satisfied, the value must be anything other than NIL.

If

((ZEROP A)9)

is satisfied (in other words A is 0) then the value of the "total" expression is 9. The minute one of the pairs is satisfied the COND function stops. If

((ZEROP A)9)

is not satisfied, the COND function looks at the next pair:

((GREATERP A C)8)

If this pair is satisfied, then the total value for the COND function expression is 8 (assuming that A is greater than C). If:

((GREATERP A C)8)

is not satisfied, the COND function looks at the last pair:

(T 0)

77

Since T is always "not" NIL the pair is satisfied and the value of the expression is 0.

Must the last pair in a COND function expression be a (T x), where x can be anything?

Yes, assuming that none of the conditions are satisfied, the COND function expression would not have a meaningful value. Therefore, the last pair (T x) is a default pair (Fig. 77). If none of the others are satisfied, then the default pair determines the value of the expression.

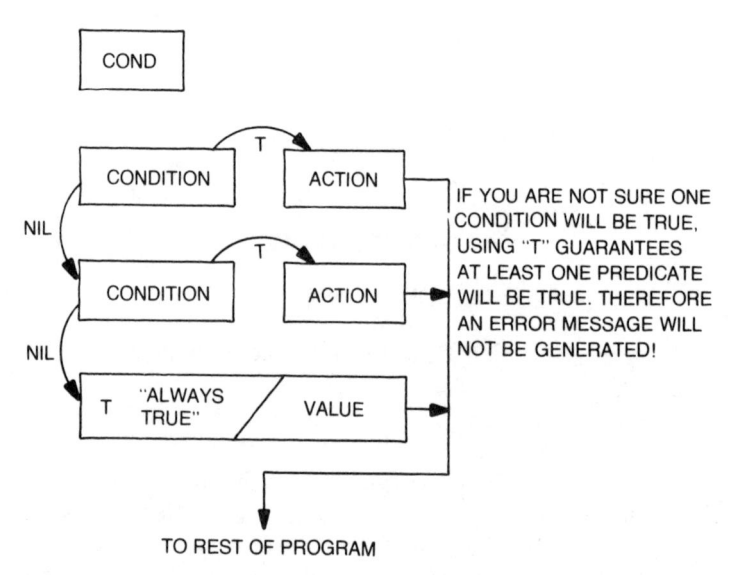

Fig. 77.

What happens if the default pair is not included and none of the condition pairs are satisfied?

LISP will respond with an error message.

RECURSIVE FUNCTIONS

What are the important things to remember about writing functions?

Before defining writing procedures, take another look at parentheses. The balance of parentheses must always be kept, no matter what type of function is being written. If there is an unbalance, the expression will not be interpreted correctly by the LISP language. You will find when you write complex expressions in LISP that many expressions end in a great quantity of right parentheses. This is normal, as they must close all the S-expressions that were left open during the writing of the "total" expression. Many programmers choose different methods to check whether they have enclosed the expression in the right amount of parentheses. One method is to count all the left parentheses and then count all the right parentheses. There should be the same number of left and right parentheses if the expression has been written correctly. Another method is to view each subexpression and ask yourself if the expression has been closed. Always remember that for every left parenthesis there must be a corresponding right parenthesis. If there is not, the LISP language will produce incorrect results—if any (Fig. 78). Take the following example and try the two methods yourself:

(DEFINE((FACT (LAMBDA (N)(COND
((ZEROP N) 1)(T (TIMES N (FACT (DIFFERENCE
N 1)))))))))

Simple observation will indicate that there are 12 left parentheses and 12 right parentheses.

The expression just given is the function for finding the factorial of any positive number. The word *fact* stands for the name of

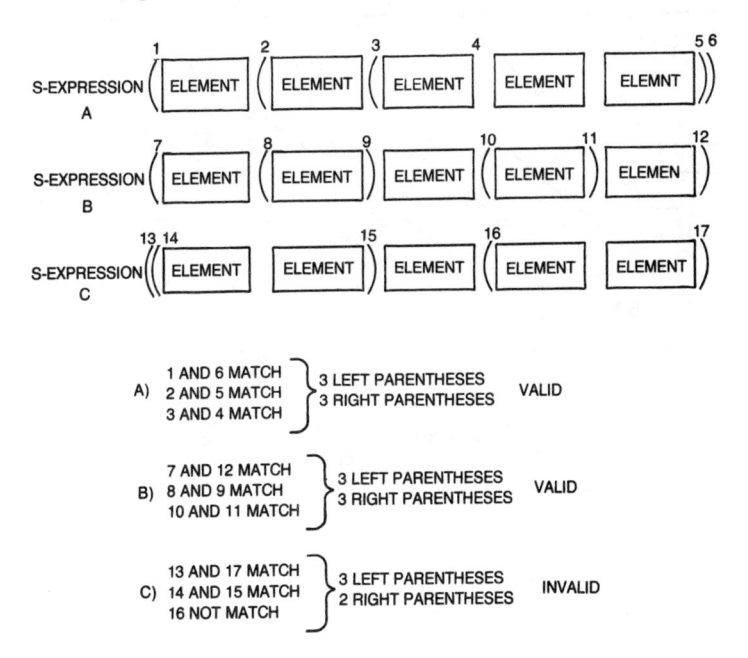

Fig. 78.

the function being defined. The LAMBDA expression declares how many arguments the function FACT will require.

Parentheses are very important in LISP. The word DEFINE is at the 0 level and must be followed by three parentheses. Separate the first two so that if more than one function is defined you can think of each function extra as being preceded by a left parenthesis. Typically, functions start with a function name, followed by LAMBDA and a list of formal arguments, then followed by COND (the conditions of the function).

What else should be noted?

If the S-expression is very lengthly, it can be written on more than one line. LISP is a free-format language. If you prefer, you can say that LISP programs are written in free-field-format. LISP only recognizes S-expressions that are correctly balanced in terms of parentheses—not in respect to what appears on what line. You can write more than one statement per line or only one statement per line. For programmers just learning LISP, limit the number of statements per line. It makes reading of the program easier if each

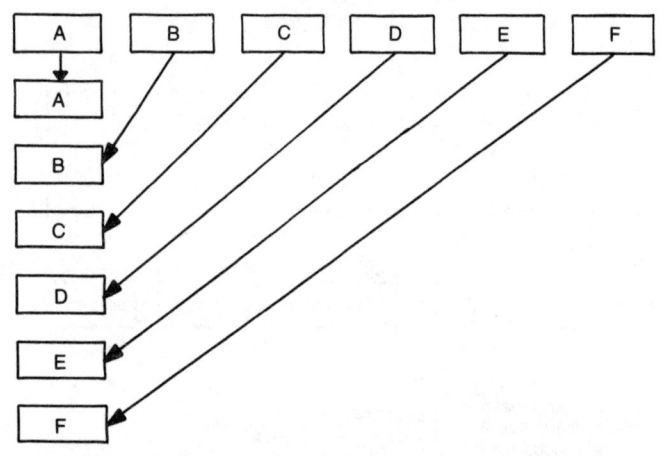

THIS METHOD OF ONE STATEMENT PER LINE INCREASES PROGRAM READABILITY AND SOFTWARE RELIABILITY. BEING ABLE TO SEE EACH STEP SINGLY INSTEAD OF AS A WHOLE VASTLY INCREASES THE ABILITY TO DEBUG PROGRAMS, PARTICULARLY IF THEY ARE LENGTHY OR COMPLEX IN NATURE.

ALSO, PRESENTING THE PROGRAM TO THE SYSTEM ON A STATEMENT PER STATEMENT BASIS CUARANTEES THAT THERE WILL BE NO ERRONEOUS MATERIAL IN THE TERMINAL BUFFER.

Fig. 79.

line contains all the essentials of the subexpression written on that line (Fig. 79).

RECURSIVE LIST PROCESSING

What are the basic LIST processing functions?
They are CONS, CAR and CDR.

When you write recursive LIST PROCESSING functions, which functions (standard) are used most often?
CAR and CDR are used most often in defining new functions that are LIST processing recursive.

How do you "create" the function ADD?
Write the following expression:
DEFINE(((ADD (LAMBDA (K) (COND
((NULL K) 0)(T(PLUS(CAR K) (ADD(CDR K)))))))))

What does the ADD function do?
The ADD function adds up the elements in a list named K.

What are some examples of the ADD function?
if K is (1 2 3 4)
Then (ADD K) is 10
if K is (34 56 78 90)
then (ADD K) is 258
if K is (3 456 7 890 5 678 89 67 4567)
then (ADD) is 6762
if K is (34 35 37 38 39804 65)
then (ADD K) is 40049

Can you do the same thing for multiplication?
Yes, you can write the following definition expression:
DEFINE (((MULT(LAMBDA (V)(COND
((NULL V)
1)(T(TIMES(CAR V)(MULT(CDR V)))))))))

What are some examples of the MULT function and what does it do?
The MULT function finds the product of the numbers in a list in the same fashion that the ADD function finds the sum of the numbers in a list. The following examples will help:
if V is (2 4 6 8)
Then (MULT V) is 384
if V is (67 4 10 8)
then (MULT V) is 21440

What happens when you apply the ADD function to a list containing sublists?

81

One of a few different things could happen. First you would inevitably get the wrong results. Second, you could also receive a LISP error message. The way the function is defined—if you tried to apply it—at some point you would try to add a list to a number. The PLUS function, used in the definition of the ADD function, cannot do this.

Can you write a function that could add the numbers in a list in cases even with sublists?

Yes, you can write a recursive function, called ADL, which would form the sum of the numbers in a list—whether sub-lists existed or not. Write it as follows:

DEFINE(((ADL(LAMBDA (G)
(COND ((NULL G)
0)
((ATOM (CAR G)) (PLUS (CAR G)
(ADL (DR G))))
(T (PLUS (ADL (CAR G))
(ADL (CDR G)))))))))

What are some examples?
if G is (3(4 5 6(7)))then
(ADL G) is 25
if G is (3 3 3 (4) 3) then
(ADL G) is 16
if G is ((6)(6)(6 6)) then
(ADL G) is 24

Can a predicate be defined recursively?

Yes, like any other function in LISP, a predicate can be defined recursively.

What is the MEMBER function?

The MEMBER function, which is a standard function in LISP, checks to see if its first argument is found present in its second argument. If the first argument is found, the MEMBER function returns a value of T. If it is not found, the MEMBER function returns a value of NIL.

What are some examples of MEMBER in operation?
Consider the following:
if A is 6 and B is (4 5 6 7)
if C is 3 and D is (8 6 5 7 8)
if E is 1 and F is (6 5 4 1 9)
if G is 5 and H is (7 6 4 8)
then
(MEMBER A B) is T

(MEMBER C D) is NIL
(MEMBER E F) is T
(MEMBER G H) is NIL

If MEMBER was not a standard function in LISP, how could it be written?

The function MEMBER could be written as:
DEFINE(((MEMBER (LAMBDA(A B)
(COND ((NULL
B) NIL) ((EQUAL A
(CAR B)) T)
(T (MEMBER A
(CDR B))))))))

Can you define more than one function at a time?

Yes, this was discussed previously. Try to define the functions ADL. MULT and MEMBER with one define expression:
DEFINE ((
(ADL (LAMBDA (A)
(COND(NULL A) 0)
(T PLUS (CAR A) (ADL
(CDR A)))))))
(MULT(LAMBDA (B)
(COND((NULL B)1
T(TIMES (CAR B)
(MULT (CDR B)))))))
(MEMBER (LAMBDA (C D)
(COND((NULL D)NIL)
((EQUAL C (CAR D))
T)(T(MEMBER C
(CDR D))))))))

LOGIC

What are the logical operators in LISP?

They are the operators AND, OR and NOT. They are quite similar to their counterparts in FORTRAN and BASIC.

What is the operator NOT?

The NOT operator has only one argument and has a value of T if its one argument is NIL. It has a value of NIL if its one argument is T. If its argument is anything other than T or NIL it also has the value NIL. Therefore, you can see on simple observation that the NOT operator reverses its argument to form its value. It should be mentioned that the NULL and the NOT are exactly identical, but LISP keeps them both (Fig. 80).

NIL ←NOT— T

T ←NOT— NIL

NIL ←NOT— ANYTHING OTHER THAN "T"

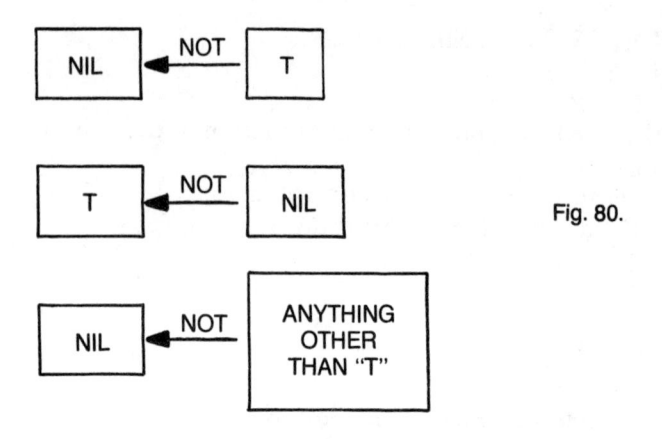

Fig. 80.

What about the AND and OR operators?

The operators AND and OR can have an indefinite number of arguments. AND operates as follows, AND is always NIL "unless" all the arguments of AND are non-NIL. Here as before, NIL means false. Therefore, non-NIL means "true," The OR operator is always true unless all its arguments are NIL. If all the arguments of AND are TRUE, then the value returned by AND is T. Similarly, the value of the OR operator is NIL if all its arguments are NIL.

What are some examples of the AND operator (Fig. 81)?

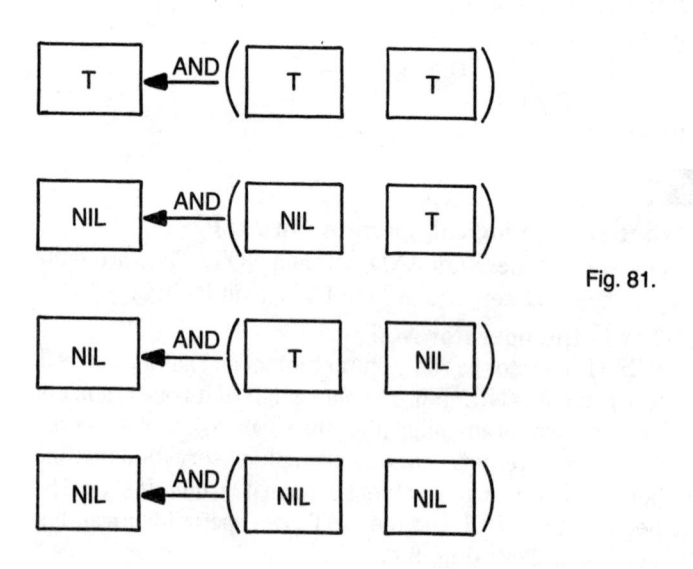

T ←AND—(T   T)

NIL ←AND—(NIL   T)

NIL ←AND—(T   NIL)

NIL ←AND—(NIL   NIL)

Fig. 81.

(AND T T) is T
(AND NIL T) is NIL
(AND T NIL) is NIL
(AND NIL NIL) is NIL
(AND T T T T) is T
(AND NIL NIL NIL) is NIL
(AND NIL NIL T T T T) is NIL

What are some examples of the OR operator (Fig. 82)?
(OR T NIL) is T
(OR T T) is T
(OR NIL T) is T
(OR NIL NIL) is NIL
(OR NIL NIL T T NIL) is T
(OR NIL NIL NIL NIL NIL) is NIL
(OR NIL T NIL NIL NIL NIL) is T

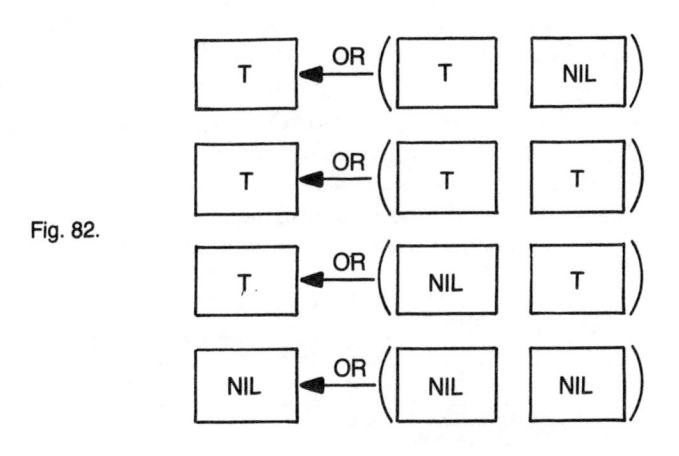

Fig. 82.

Can you use the OR operation to create a function?
Yes, the perfect example would to use the OR to improve the MEMBER function. The MEMBER function, as it is now, can only determine if its first argument is a member of the given LIST. By using the OR you can extend the operation of the MEMBER function to be able to handle LISTS with sub-LISTS within them.

How would you write this better version of the MEMBER function?
Write it as:
(DEFINE ((
(MEMBER (LAMBDA (A B)
(COND((NULL B)

85

NIL)(T OR(COND((ATOM(CAR B))
(EQUAL A(CAR B)))
(T(MEMBER A(CAR B))))
(MEMBER A(CDR B)))))))))

Can AND, NOT and OR be thought as of predicates?

Yes, since their values are always T or NIL. However, they are different from other predicates because their arguments, as well as their values are normally either T or NIL.

DOT NOTATION

What is DOT NOTATION?

The LIST (X.Y) is a list of two elements in LISP, but it must not be confused with the LIST (X Y). The pair of elements X Y are pointers when written as (X.Y).

Can pointers be explained better?

To understand dotted pairs, which is what (X.Y) are, you must understand how lists are handled in the memory of the computer. Memory refers to the mechanism that actively stores the lists during program execution. In the LISP language, a list consists of a sequence of pairs. The first element of each pair is a pointer to an ATOM or a pointer to a sublist (a list within a list). The second element of each pair is a pointer to the next pair of elements. DOT NOTATION allows you to look at the pairs separately (Fig. 83).

NIL IS A SPECIAL POINTER THAT POINTS TO THE END OF THE LIST.

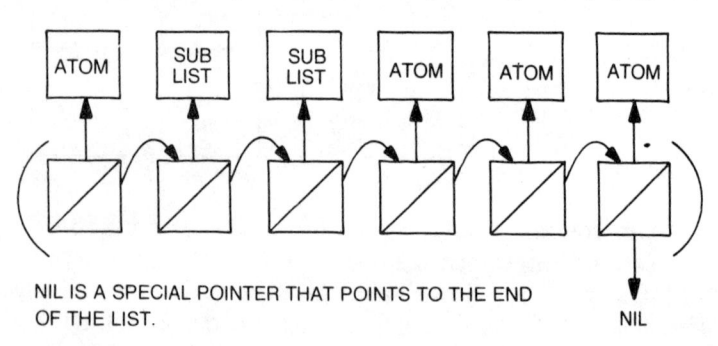

Fig. 83.

What is a dotted pair?

(X.Y) is a single pair. Its first element, X, is a pointer to an ATOM or a sub-LIST named X. Its second element is a pointer to the next pair Y.

How is the list (XY) formed using the information given?

The list (X Y) would be formed in a quite different way. First of all, there is a need for two pairs to be involved. The first pair would be the pointer to X, while the second pair would be a pointer to Y. But don't forget the first pointer must also point to the second pair. Of course, the second element of the first pair points to the second pair. The second element of the second pair must point to the next pair, if you use the definition given so far. In many cases, the second element will contain zero, as in many cases in LISP LIST processing situations.

Why would the second element contain zero?

To denote the end of a list. In LISP, the second element would never contain zero, but rather NIL and it would be a special pointer that pointed to the end of a list. This special pointer written in DOT NOTATION would be:

(Y.NIL)

How would a list be shown?

In DOT NOTATION you can write:

(X.(Y.NIL))

How would you write a list containing sublists in DOT NOTATION?

It would be written as:

(Q.((W.(E.NIL)).NIL))

assuming that the list was

(Q(W E))

How do you interpret what you just wrote in DOT NOTATION about sublists?

This first pair would be the pointer to Q and a pointer to the second pair. The second pair would be a pointer to (W E) and a pointer to NIL.

What is meant by a pointer to (W E)?

This means a pointer to the first pair in the representation of (W E). This pair is, of course, a pointer to W and a pointer to the second pair.

Why is this so extremely important in LISP?

The convention that a pointer to the first of a set of pairs representing a list can be taken as a pointer to the list itself leads to a proper explanation and understanding of the fundamental functions CAR, CONS and CDR.

THE GENERAL LIST

What is a general list in LISP?
Any list in the form of:
(A B C D E F G H I J K)

where any of the symbols A B C D E F G H I J K can stand for ATOMS or sublists. The first pair in the representation of this list is a pointer to A and a pointer to the second pair. The remaining pairs beginning with the second pair are in exactly the same format as if the list was:
(B C D E F G H I J K)
instead of
(A B C D E F G H I J K).

A pointer to the second pair in the original list can therefore be considered as a pointer to the list:
(B C D E F G H I J K)
or to the representation of the list.

What is the general definition of a list.

A list is represented in memory by a pair consisting of a pointer to (CAR A) and a pointer to (CDR A), assuming the name of the list is A. Since the definition is recursive you should interpret the above not to mean that a list is represented by only one, and only one pair. This is because (CAR A) and CDR A) will themselves be represented by pairs. This defintion is the real reason why CAR and CDR are so important in LISP (Fig. 84).

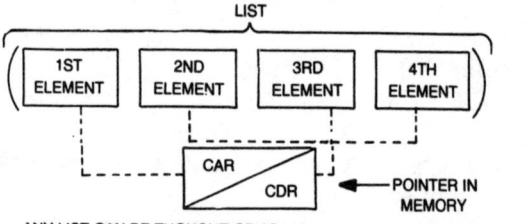

Fig. 84.

ANY LIST CAN BE THOUGHT OF AS THE PAIR POINTING TO THE CAR AND TO THE CDR OR THE LIST.

In DOT NOTATION how can you represent the functions CAR and CDR?

If Z is (X.Y) then (CAR Z) is X and (CDR Z) is B
also
if Z is (X.Y) then (CONS X Y) is C.

When can you use DOT NOTATION in a LISP program?

DOT NOTATION can be used anywhere within a LISP function or program for the creation of temporary lists and for various other purposes. It uses less memory space than list notation, but you must always remember that only two quantities can be dotted at a time. The following has absolutely no meaning in LISP:

(S.D.F.H)   but as shown before you   (S.(D.P))
(X.Y.Z)   can write: (X.(Y.Z))

Every list that exists in LISP that can be expressed as an S-expression can be converted to DOT NOTATION. *Caution:* not every expression in DOT NOTATION can be expressed as LIST NOTATION (standard notation used in S-expresssions).

TWO LIST RECURSION

How much difference is there between two list recursion and single list recursion?

The construction of functions for two list recursion is quite the same as the construction of functions using only one list.

The LISP system function APPEND does what?

It appends two lists, such as in the following cases:
If A is (3 4 5) and B is (4)
if C is (7 6) and D is (7 6 5)
if E is (4 5 6) and F is (3)
then
(APPEND A B) is (3 4 5 4)
(APPEND C D) is (7 6 7 6 5)
(APPEND E F) is (4 5 6 3)

How do you define APPEND in LISP?
DEFINE((
(APPEND(LAMBDA (X Y)
(COND((NULL
X)Y)(T(CONS(CAR X)
(APPEND (CDR X)
Y))))))))

Using the idea of two list recursion, can EQUAL be redefined?
DEFINE((
(EQUAL(LAMBDA (X Y)
(COND((NULL X)
(NULL Y))((ATOM X)(AND
(ATOM Y) (EQ X Y)))
((ATOM Y)NIL)(T
(AND(EQUAL(CAR X)
(CAR Y))
(EQUAL(CDR X)(CDR Y)))) provides a simpler and faster method that works on ATOMS only—with respect to EQUAL.

TYPE FUNCTIONS

What is a type function?

You have already used a type function—the function ATOM. Basically, a type function determines what kind of a variable, a number or other item is.

How do you determine if a variable is a number orp or not?
Use the predicate NUMBERP.
What are some examples of the use of NUMBERP?
if A is 5
if C is T(the symbol)
if H is (T)
if J is (4 5 6)
if K is 2345
then
(NUMBERP A) is T
(NUMBERP C) is NIL
(NUMBERP H) is NIL
(NUMBERP J) is NIL
(NUMBERP K) is T

NUMBERP applies to numbers and ATOM applies to ATOMS. Are there any other "type" functions?
Yes, there are two more and they both deal with numbers. They are FIXP and FLOATP.
What does FIXP do?
FIXP determines whether a number is a fixed point (integer) or not.
What are some examples?
if A is 34.9
if B is 45
if C is 56.98
if D is 2345.9
if E is 34
then
(FIXP A) is NIL
(FIXP B) is T
(FIXP C) is NIL
(FIXP D) is NIL
(FIXP E) is T

What does FLOATP do?
FLOATP tests whether a number is in floating point or not. It tests whether there is anything to the right of the decimal point or not, "whether it is an integer or not." In essence, it is the opposite of FIXP.
What are some examples of FLOATP?
if A is 89
if B is 5.87

if C is 76
if D is 56.03
if E is 2345
then
(FLOATP A) is NIL
(FLOATP B) is T
(FLOATP C) is NIL
(FLOATP D) is T
(FLOATP E) is NIL

Is there an important function that can be constructed from FLOATP and FIXP?

Yes, it is called COUNTFIXFLOAT. COUNTFIXFLOAT returns as its value a list of two integers. The first integer in the list is the number of fixed point numbers on the list which is the argument of COUNTFIXFLOAT. The second integer represents the number of floating point numbers in the list which is the argument.

What are some examples of how it operates?

if A is ((45 3.8)((34.9 56)(56.9))8)
if B is (4.9 67 34.98 6.9 89 7)
if C is (34 (56.9 56.8) 4)
if D is (4(6(56.8(65.9(56)))))
then
(COUNTIFIXFLOAT A) is (3 3)
(COUNTFIXFLOAT B) is (3 3)
(COUNTFIXFLOAT C) is (2 2)
(COUNTIFIXFLOAT D) is 3 2)

How would you write the expression definition for COUNTFIXFLOAT?

DEFINE((
(COUNTIFIXFLOAT(LAMBDA (X)
(COND((NULL X)
(QUOTE (0 0)))
((ATOM X)(COND((NOT
(NUMBERP X))(QUOTE (0 0)))
((FIXP X)(QUOTE (1 0)))
((FLOATP X)(QUOTE (0 1)))(T
(QUOTE (0 0)))))
(T(SUMM(COUNTFIXFLOAT(
CAR X)) (COUNTFIXFLOAT(
CDR X)))))))

What is the function called SUMM?

It is a subroutine used by COUNTFIXFLOAT. This function adds the two lists of numbers—integers and non-integers—on an element by element basis. Also, it must be included with the definition, of COUNTFIXFLOAT. To finish the COUNTFIX-FLOAT definition, here is the section that contains the SUMM function:

(SUMM(LAMBDA(X Y)(CONS
(PLUS (CAR X)
(CAR Y)) (LIST(PLUS(CADR X)
(CADR Y))))))))

Note that the expression given above is an integral part of the COUNTFIXFLOAT definition and must not be separated when used in actual practice. In using this function of COUNTFIXFLOAT, the SUMM subroutine is written as it is directly after the last line in the preceding section on how to write the expression.

MORE REVIEW

In the following example, which variables are bound and which are free?
(LAMBDA(X Y Z)(TIMES(PLUS X Z)(PLUS Y W)(MINUS U)))
X Y Z are bound while W U are free.
What is the value of:
(CAR(QUOTE (A B C)))
A
What is the value of: (PLUS 3(CAR(QUOTE (5 6))))6))))
8
What is the value of: (CDR(LIST(QUOTE(4 6))3)
(3 9 7 4)
What is the value of:
(CONS(QUOTE MIC)(LIST(QUOTE E)))
(MIC E)
If the function CDDR was applied to (4 5 6 7), what is the value?
(6 7)
If the function CAADR is applied to (6((7)2 4)), what is the value?
7
Translate into DOT NOTATION
((X)Y)
((X.NIL).(Y.NIL))
Translate into DOT NOTATION

(X(Y)Z(A B))
(X.((Y.NIL).(Z.((A.(B.NIL)).NIL))))

Translate into DOT NOTATION the following: (((Q)R S)T U)
(((Q.NIL).(R.(S.NIL))).(T.(U.NIL)))

Translate into list notation:
(S.(T.(U.NIL)))
(S T U)

Translate into list notation:
(NIL.(Y.NIL))
(NIL Y)

Translate into list notation:
(Q.(W.((E.(R.((T.NIL).NIL))).NIL)))
(QW(ER(T)))

What is the value of:
(NUMBERP(DIFFERENCE 10(QUOTIENT 20 4)))
T

What is the value of:
(NUMBERP(CAR(QUOTE(PLUS 3 4))))
NIL

What is the value of:
(NUMBERP -9)
T

PROGRAMMING

How is a LISP program written?

It is written so that it can replace a function or the description of a function.

How is this done?

This is done by using the special function PROG (everything in LISP is done with functions) which can have an indefinite number of arguments.

Where is the PROG function usually found?

A PROG expression is generally the second argument of a LAMBDA expression. It can also be used elsewhere.

What are the arguments of a PROG expression?

They are DECLARATION, STATEMENTS, LABELS, TRANSFERS, CONDITIONALS and RETURNING VALUES (Fig. 85).

What are declarations?

They are the first argument of PROG and they are a list of the variables that occur in that PROG. These variables are called programming variables and must be defined, but they do not have

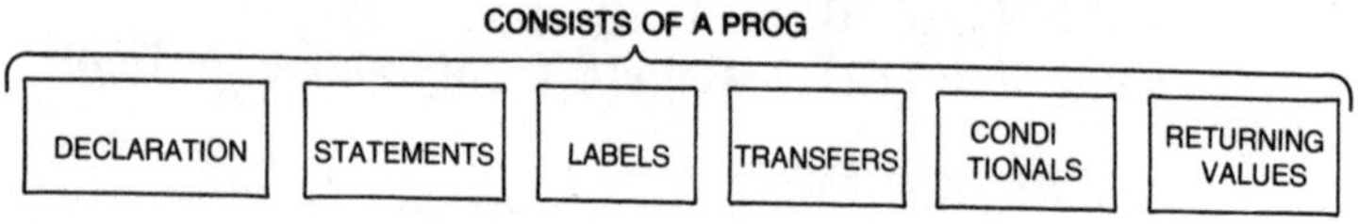

```
                      CONSISTS OF A PROG
   ┌─────────────────────────────────────────────────────────┐
   ┌─────────┐ ┌──────────┐ ┌──────┐ ┌─────────┐ ┌───────┐ ┌──────────┐
   │DECLARATION│ │STATEMENTS│ │LABELS│ │TRANSFERS│ │ CONDI-│ │ RETURNING│
   │         │ │          │ │      │ │         │ │TIONALS│ │  VALUES  │
   └─────────┘ └──────────┘ └──────┘ └─────────┘ └───────┘ └──────────┘
```

Fig. 85.

to be defined as integer or floating point, etc. Variables tend to change type during program execution. As usual, any variable can represent a list.

What are statements?

Statements are expressions like assignment (SETQ, SET), subroutine calls. These are simply expressions that use the name of the subroutine as functions in expressions.

What are labels?

Labels are always single ATOMS and are distinguished from functions by the fact that they are ATOMS.

What is a transfer?

A transfer is like a GO TO statement. In LISP, it is the GO function and it has one argument, a label (Fig. 86). For example:
(GO RESULTS)
(GO START)
(GO DIGIT)

What are conditionals?

Remember the COND function—similar to the IF statement in other languages. COND is different in functions and in programs. In functions, it has as a quantity its second element of each pair. But in a program, its second element of each pair is a statement (any statement that is legal in LISP). Also in a program, the last pair of elements do not have to be a T. Which means if each pair of elements (arguments) are nil, then the next statement is executed.

What is VALUE RETURNING?

To return a value, use the return function. It has only one argument, the value that is to be returned. An example would be:
(RETURN K).

Can you write a short program using the statements just discussed?

Yes, write the following program defining factorials:
DEFINE(((FACT(LAMBDA (N) (PROG (I J)
(SETQ I N) (SETQ J1)
K(COND((ZEROP I)(GO L)))
(SETQ J(TIMES J I))

```
(SETQ I (DIFFERENCE I 1))
(GO K)
L(RETURN J) ))))
```

Notice the five right parentheses after the last statement. In general, three parentheses are used if more definitions are to come within the same DEFINE expression and five right parentheses if otherwise.

MORE ON PROGRAMMING

How do you construct LISTS?

When you write a program in LISP that produces a list as its value, it is important to produce the list in the right order and in the

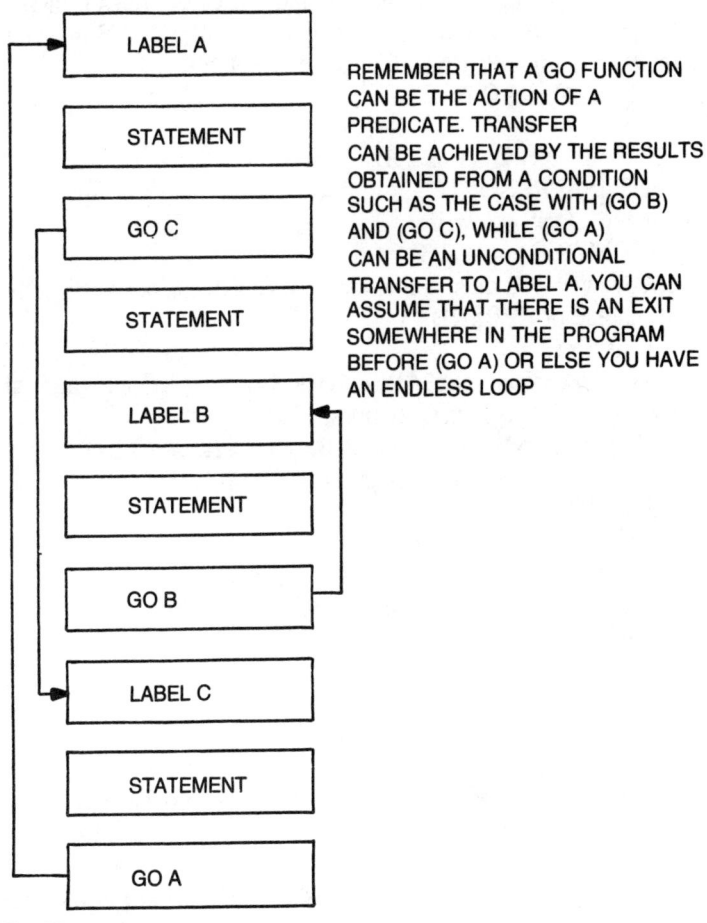

REMEMBER THAT A GO FUNCTION CAN BE THE ACTION OF A PREDICATE. TRANSFER CAN BE ACHIEVED BY THE RESULTS OBTAINED FROM A CONDITION SUCH AS THE CASE WITH (GO B) AND (GO C), WHILE (GO A) CAN BE AN UNCONDITIONAL TRANSFER TO LABEL A. YOU CAN ASSUME THAT THERE IS AN EXIT SOMEWHERE IN THE PROGRAM BEFORE (GO A) OR ELSE YOU HAVE AN ENDLESS LOOP

Fig. 86.

right direction. It is more efficient when you are building lists to begin with the last element and add each element in front of it and finally adding the first element of the list last.

The reason for this is that LISP keeps track at all times where the beginning of each list is, but LISP does not keep track of where the end is for each list. If you are putting elements onto the end of a list, you must go down the list from the first element to the last element searching for the last element. If you don't know where the last element is, you cannot place something after it.

The function generally used to place elements onto a list is CONS. Use the CONS function rather than the APPEND function in writing programs. It is true that APPEND can put elements onto the front (beginning) or the end of a list, but CONS does it faster and places it at the beginning of the list. Actually, CONS is much faster than using APPEND. To use APPEND:
if S is (4) and Q is (2 3)
then
(APPEND S Q) is (4 2 3)
while (APPEND Q S) is (2 3 4)
using CONS we write:
(CONS S Q) is (4 2 3)

However, you must remember that CONS can not be directly used instead of APPEND.

Why not?

The first argument of APPEND is always a LIST and the first argument of CONS is usually not a LIST.

Can you write a program that reverses a LIST?
Yes, using the CONS function:
DEFINE ((
(REVERSE(LAMBDA (A)
(PROG (X Y)
(SETQ X A)(SETQ Y NIL)
K(COND((NULL X)(RETURN Y)))
SETQ Y(CONS
(CAR X)Y))
(SETQ X (CDR X))
(GO K))))))

What is one of the curious things about LISP?

The most efficient way to create a list is from back to front, yet the most efficient way to use a list is from front to back (Fig. 87)

What is the name of the LISP functions that construct lists from lists?

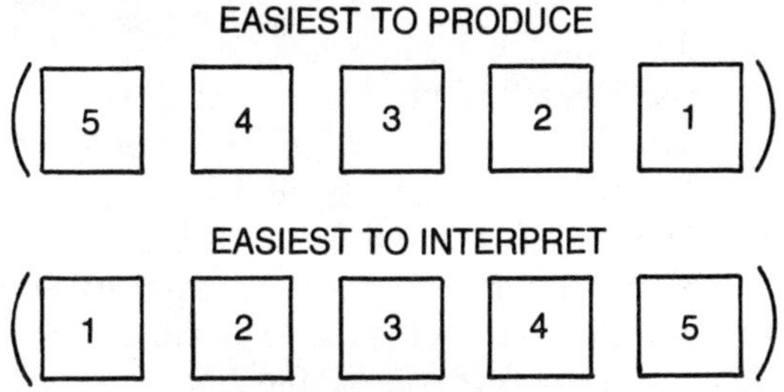

EASIEST TO PRODUCE

Fig. 87.

([5] [4] [3] [2] [1])

EASIEST TO INTERPRET

([1] [2] [3] [4] [5])

They are the MAP functions. MAPCAR is a function that has two arguments, the first argument denotes a list and the second argument is the name of another function. MAPCAR applies the named function to the elements of the list and produces as its value a list of the results. Specifically, MAPCAR applies the function so named as its second argument to:

(CAR L)
(CADR L)
(CADDR L)
(CADDDR L)
(CADDDDR L)
(CADDDDDR L)

and so forth, with these being the elements of the list L.

Are there other MAP functions?

Yes, for example there is MAPLIST. MAPLIST also has two arguments. The first is a list and the second is a function that is applied to the elements of the list. However, there is a difference. MAPLIST applies the function named to the list itself first, then to:

(CDR L)
(CDDR L)
(CDDDR L)
(CDDDDR L)
(CDDDDDR L)

and so on.

How can you represent arrays in LISP?

Use a list of lists. If you want the matrix:

1 2 3 4 5 6 7 8 9
2 3 4 5 6 7 8 9 1
3 4 5 6 7 8 9 1 2
4 5 6 7 8 9 1 2 3
5 6 7 8 9 1 2 3 4
6 7 8 9 1 2 3 4 5
7 8 9 1 2 3 4 5 6

8 9 1 2 3 4 5 6 7
9 1 2 3 4 5 6 7 8
which is a 9×9 matrix you can write:
((1 2 3 4 5 6 7 8 9) (2 3 4 5 6 7 8 9 1)(3 4 5 6 7 8 9 1 2)
(4 5 6 7 8 9 1 2 3)(5 6 7 8 9 1 2 3 4) (6 7 8 9 1 2 3 4 5)
(7 8 9 1 2 3 4 5 6)(8 9 1 2 3 4 5 6 7)(9 1 2 3 4 5 6 7 8))

Can you write a program to set up such a list like the one in the preceding example?
Yes, using the GREATERP function:
```
DEFINE((
(MAT(LAMBDA (N) (PROG
(I J K L Z)
SETQ J N) (SETQ K NIL)
B(COND((EQUAL I J)
(SETQ Z 1))
(T(SETQ Z 0)))
SETQ K(CONS ZK))
SETQ J(DIFFERENCE J 1))
(COND((GREATERP J 0)
(GO B)))
(SETQ L (CONS K L))
((SETQ I (DIFFERENCE I 1))
(COND((GREATERP I 0)
(GO A)))
(RETURN L) )))))
```

What is the difference between a function's effect and value?

The effect is what the function does to variables, such as changing their value. Value is the value returned by a function without changing the values of any of the variables it has used. In LISP, many of the standard functions can be used for effect and for their value. They can be used to change the value of some variable or they can be used to produce some value. For example, the following expressions using standard functions only produce a value in the way they are written:
(CAR L)
(CDR L)
(CONS E R)
(DIFFERENCE K L)
(TIMES F G)
(PLUS J K)
(QUOTIENT I P)

In each case shown, the variables used by the functions are not changed, but observe the following functions (expressions):
(SET A B)
(SETQ R T)
These functions change the value of the variables they are using. In other words, they have an effect on the variables.

Can predicates be used in programs?
Yes, when a predicate is used in a program it simply returns a value of either T or NIL. Programs that return T and NIL are likely to return T and NIL in a manner such that T is returned in one place and NIL is returned in another place. Of course, in LISP, like other programming languages, you can have more than one return function in it.

What is a recursive program in LISP?
A recursive program in LISP is like any other recursive program in any other language that supports recursiveness. A recursive program is either a program that calls itself, or it is one of a group of programs that call themselves one after the othe. in a cyclic fashion.

LISP programs tend to be more recursive than programs written in other languages, primarily because LISP operates upon lists. It should be quite understandable that LISP programs that operate on lists are "not as recursive" as the functions themselves that operate on lists. This is because a LISP program will usually use looping, where the corresponding LISP function will use recursion to the same end. However, the treatment of sublists by a program (assuming sublists of a list) is usually explicitly recursive. A corresponding non-recursive program would require the use of a push-down list and would therefore be more cumbersome.

Can you rewrite the ADL function (see recursive list processing) as a program?
Yes, and you can also reduce one level of recursiveness at the same time:
(DEFINE((
(ADL(LAMBDA (L)(PROG(M N X)
(SETQ M L) (SETQ N 0)
A(COND((NULL M)
(RETURN N)))
(SETQ X (CAR M))
(SETQ M (CDR M))
(COND((ATOM X)
(SETQ N (PLUS N X)))

(T (SETQ N (PLUS N (ADL X)))))
(GO A))))))
The above program is typical of LISP.

Can you write a program inside another program?

Yes, however, every time PROG is used it requires a certain amount of time that is unavoidable. Even if there are no new variables, you must still look (LISP language) for them. Also, this is not a particularly efficient way of programming. In LISP, there is another function called PROGN. It is almost like a compound statement in ALGOL. Speaking of ALGOL, the LISP function PROG is like a block in ALGOL.

What is PROGN?

PROGN has an indefinite number of arguments. Each of these arguments are statements is a LISP program. The only purpose of PROGN is to bring these statements together into a single statement. There is one important restriction, "labels" are not allowed with the use of PROGN. Like any other function in the LISP language, PROGN has a value. Its value is *always* the value of its last argument. Therefore, you can readily see that PROGN can be used not only for its effect, but also for its value. This PROGN function can be used to form WHERE expressions which occur in some algebraic languages, but not in FORTRAN or ALGOL.

What is the PROG2 function?

The PROGN function is an extension of the PROG2 function, which has only two arguments. As with the PROGN function, PROG2's value is that of its last argument. Some LISP language systems have PROG2 but not PROGN functions.

What is an example using PROGN function?

To demonstrate properly, write a more complex program, even iif it is not any longer in length. Call the program MAX, and do the following. MAX will accept two lists, one of which is numeric the other is a list of ATOMS (the numeric list is actually a list of numeric ATOMS). MAX will ascertain the largest numeric value from the list of numerics and then select the ATOM from the ATOM list which occupies the same relative spot. For example, if the numeric list is:

(4 6 3 8 9)

the largest value is 9 and it is in the 5th position in the list.

You also need a list of ATOMS such as:

(B O O K S)

This program will use S because it also occupies the last (fifth) place. The program is written as follows:

```
DEFINE((
(MAX(LAMBDA (J K )(PROG
(T U R S W X)
(SETQ T (CAR J))
(SETQ U(CAR K))
(SETQ R(CDR J))
A(COND((NULL R)
RETURN U)))
(SETQ W (CAR R))
(SETQ X (CAR S))
(SETQ R(CDR R))
(SETQ S (CDR S))
(COND((GREATERP W T)
(PROGN(SETQ T W)(SETQ U X))))
(GO A) )))))
```

Of course, PROGN in this program could have been replaced by PROG2.

The PROGN does what?

The PROGN function evaluates its arguments.

What does evaluate a function mean?

If you say evaluate TIMES (9 7) you are actually finding the value. But, if you say evaluate a function in LISP it means execute the function. The use of functions for their effect makes this distinction necessary. If the expression:

(SETQ A B)

is to be evaluated you are not just asking for the value, which of course is the value of B, but you also want its effect. The expression

(SETQ A B)

has the effect of setting A to B.

If you where talking about an arithmetic function instead, you would probably mean find the value if you said evaluate a function.

What is the evaluation rule in LISP?

To evaluate a function F in the normal manner, its arguments, both atoms and function uses, are evaluated in order—from left to right. The definition of F is applied to this list of values, producing the value of F.

Why must the uses of AND be watched carefully?

The AND function is noncommutative.

What does evaluation have to do with the DEFINE function?

The evaluation rule holds for all functions and programs that are defined by the DEFINE function. This rule does have some important exceptions.

What are the exceptions?

AND and OR are evaluated in a different way. When evaluating: (AND A B)

evaluate A and then test it to see if it is NIL. If so, then the value of:

(AND A B)

is NIL and there is no need to evaluate B. Only if the value of A is T should you evaluate B.

Why can't you use AND instead of PROGN or PROG2 in a program?

If you write:

(AND(SETQ A B)(SETQ C D))

instead of:

(PROG2(SETQ A B)(SETQ C D))

it would work most of the time, unless B has a value of NIL. If it did have a value of NIL you would never get to:

(SETQ C D)

How about OR?

The evaluation of OR is the reverse of AND. If you write:

(OR A B)

which is the reverse of:

(AND A B)

evaluate A if it is NIL then evaluate B, otherwise A is T.

The expression:

(OR A B)

is true or T and B is not evaluated.

What is the rule about AND and OR?

The use of AND and OR, with more than one argument, proceeds from left to right until an argument in the AND expression is found to be NIL or an argument in the OR expression is found to be T(Fig. 88).

How about other evaluations?

If you have a varible whose value is a list, with an S-expression indicating that it can be treated as a usage of a function (the first element of the list is a function name and the other elements are arguments) and you want to evaluate or find the value of the function as applied to those given arguments, you can use the EVAL function.

What are some examples of EVAL?

102

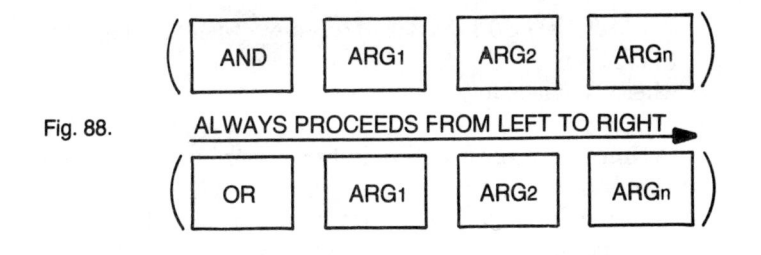

Fig. 88. ALWAYS PROCEEDS FROM LEFT TO RIGHT

if A is (PLUS 3 4)
if B is (DIFFERENCE 6 3)
if C is (LIST 5 6 7 8)
if D is (QUOTE MICE)
then
(EVAL A) is 7
(EVAL B) is 3
(EVAL C) is (5 6 7 8)
(EVAL D) is MICE

Is there a difference between (EVAL (PLUS 3 4)) and (EVAL A) where A is (PLUS 3 4)?

Yes, they are not the same. Because:
(EVAL(PLUS 3 4))
actually has the value 7, but not for the obvious reason. If you write
(DIFFERENCE 10(PLUS 3 4))
the answer 3 is the same as:
(DIFFERENCE 10 7)
so in a way:
(EVAL(PLUS 3 4))
is like:
(EVAL 7)
When you evaluate an expression like:
(EVAL 7)
you get what seems to be the correct answer because the value of 7 is obviously 7. The value of any integer is the integer itself).

If you write:
(EVAL(LIST(QUOTE MINUS)6))
The value is -6(not (MINUS 6) because the value of:
(LIST(QUOTE MINUS)6) is:
(MINUS 6) and the value of that is -6. To insure that you avoid confusion when using the EVAL function you can write it:

103

(EVAL(QUOTE(PLUS 3 3 4))) when we wish to refer to:
(EVAL A)
where A stands for:
(PLUS 3 4)

Is there another function in any other language that is like the EVAL function?

Not in most, FORTRAN, BASIC, PL/1 and ALGOL have absolutely nothing like it.

Why is EVAL so important?

The EVAL function makes LISP much more powerful than most other algebraic languages. With EVAL you can execute statements that have been constructed by the LISP program. These constructions can be different each and every time the program is run. In most algebraic languages, the form of the statements must be constructed at the beginning of the program and can not be changed in the middle. They especially cannot change during program execution, while you can change statements in LISP during execution of a program. This makes LISP a very interesting language when you deal with artificial intelligence or heuristics (self-learning program), because the program can modify itself during run-time.

Is there an analog of EVAL in any other language?

Yes, the CODE function of SNOBOL 4 is like EVAL.

What is EVALQUOTE in LISP?

EVALQUOTE is like EVAL except EVALQUOTE has two arguments instead of having only one argument instead of having only one argument like EVAL. The first argument is the name of a function, while the other is a list of its arguments. This function is another exception to the general evaluation rule.

Why is that?

The arguments of EVALQUOTE are not evaluated, but are taken in exactly the way they are "quoted." The function EVALQUOTE quotes its arguments. This is like SETQ, which quotes only its arguments rather than evaluting them.

Does this help explain the use of functions at the 0-level?

Yes, the reason for the special handling of parentheses at the 0 level in LISP is a direct outcome of the information given so far. The EVALQUOTE function is constructed partly for the special needs of LISP with regards to the LISP system which reads functions and their arguments from cards or from a terminal. The two S-expressions that are read at the same time by this part of the

LISP system (which is called the LISP supervisor) are exactly the two arguments of EVALQUOTE. In LISP, the supervisor is an extremely simple program where other languages require very complex supervisors. All the supervisor in LISP has to do is call the function EVALQUOTE over and over. Each time EVALQUOTE will read a pair of arguments from the input device. This supervisor is called the EVALQUOTE SUPERVISOR and almost all LISP systems have it. Here again you can see that LISP is truly a functional language. The supervisor itself has been constructed as a function in LISP.

What else can the EVAl function do?

The EVAL function can evaluate not only single statements, but it can evaluate actual whole programs. A program is usually rather long and complex. A single statement which constructs a program from a rather large list structure is difficult to analyze. To make things easier, you can use variables to represent list structures. These variables can be combined so that the list structures they represent becomes larger and larger until you have completed the program "statement" from these variables.

What is the FOR function in LISP?

The FOR function is the analog of the DO statement in FORTRAN and the FOR statement in ALGOL. Write the FOR function as:

(FOR A B C D Define the FOR function so that the value of the FOR function is a list of statements which could appear in a LISP program and which corresponds to repeating the list of statements which is the value of DESCRIPTION for A starting at the value B and increasing with a step size C until reaching a maximum value D.

Assume that the DESCRIPTION is a list of the arguments of PROG, not including the first argument of course, which are the variables to be defined. The value of:

(FOR A B C D DESCRIPTION)

will then also be a list of the arguments of PROG.

Are there any difficulties using the FOR function?

Yes, there is one very important problem with the construction of the FOR function. This is in choosing the names for the labels X and Y. How do you know that the symbols X and Y themselves have not been already been used as labels in the piece of the program represented by the DESCRIPTION? You don't. Also, you can call the FOR function more than once or several times and then combine the smaller pieces of program into one large piece of program. You certainly don't want the labels to repeat themselves. Duplication of labels can indeed cause problems.

What can you do?

You can use the LISP function GENSYM. This function generates a symbol that is different from every other symbol generated so far. GENSYM requires no arguments and can be used as often as desired. Always remember that it will generate a new symbol every time it is called.

Can you define the FOR function in terms of other functions?

Yes, you can write the program that follows:
DEFINE((
(FOR(LAMBDA(A B C D E) (PROG(F G H I)
(SETQ G (APPEND E (LIST
(LIST(QUOTE SETQ)
A (LIST(QUOTE PLUS)A C)))))
(SETQ H(GENSYM))
(SETQ I(GENSYM))
(SETQ G (APPEND G
(LIST(LIST(QUOTE GO)
H)I)))
(SETQF(LIST(LIST(QUOTE
SETQ) A B)
H(LIST(QUOTE COND)
(LIST(LIST(QUOTE
GREATERP)A D)
(LIST(QUOTE GO)
I)))))
(RETURN(APPEND F G)))))))

INPUT/OUTPUT

What are statements like that read and write data in LISP?

They are just like any other statements in LISP. They are functions with arguments just like other functions with arguments. Of course, it is not required to use any input/output statements at all to use LISP to solve a problem. All you have to do is define a function and then call this function ith arguments if they are necessary. LISP will automatically print the results. If there are no arguments, call the function with an opening and closing parentheses.

Are there special functions for input/output?
Yes, they are designed to complete the LISP language and to make LISP easier to use in programming.
What are these functions?
They are READ, PRINT and TERPRI.
What is the READ function?
The read function has no arguments. Every time the READ function is called, the LISP system reads one entire S-expression. In other words, it reads a non-blank character. If this character is not a left parenthesis is is assumed to be the start of an ATOM. The LISP operating system then continues to read until it reaches a blank character, or other separation character which signals to LISP that it is at the end of the ATOM being read. If the first character read was a left parenthesis symbol, LISP will continue to read until it has reached the end of the S-expression. Of course, it is counting parentheses levels to make certain it does not read too little or too much.

Does this system have a disadvantage?
Unfortunately, this is one place in LISP where there is a serious disadvantage. If there is a single error in an input line, either from a terminal or from a card reader, that error might inhibit further reading of data or input lines. This is especially true if the error happens to be a missing right parentheses from any where in the input line. Assuming there are no errors, the value of the READ function is the resulting S-expression.

What about the PRINT function?
The PRINT function has one argument. It prints the S-expression of that argument. If you use the PRINT function at the 0-level, the S-expression is printed twice.

Why is it printed twice?
The reason is that PRINT and READ, besides being used for an effect such as printing or reading data, also have values. The value is the value of the argument of the function. Therefore, if you set A equal to (6 7 8 9) and then write:
PRINT(A)
At the 0-level, the first thing that occurs is that A is printed—as it should be—since PRINT is the printing function. But then LISP does as it always does at the 0-level. It prints out the value of the called function. This problem disappears when PRINT is used inside a program.
Why is PRINT used instead of RETURN?

Print is generally used to output a temporary value, perhaps in the middle of a computation.

Is there more about PRINT?

If you print a time sharing system, usually only the PRINT function is required to output information to the user's terminal. However, with the use of a line printer, an entire line is printed at one time. If you use PRINT during the execution of a program, most of the output will appear considerably after the PRINT function was executed. This is because most line printers require a memory buffer to be filled first before a line is printed. This buffer is a small memory within the printer that holds a full line of characters for the printer. The problem is that after the program has terminated there is usually still some print information in the line "buffer."

How do you get this information printed?

Use the LISP function called TERPRI. TERPRI, which is an acronym for terminate printing, prints these characters. It is used primarily at the end of a LISP program, but it can be used in other places.

Where else can TERPRI be used?

Generally, it is used before a PRINT function. By using TERPRI before a PRINT function, you insure that a new line will be printed.

AND MORE REVIEW

Is HOUSE an ATOM?
Yes, because it is a string of characters.
Is MICE an ATOM?
Yes
Is 6789 an ATOM?
Yes, becuase it is a string of characters.
Is 45BIG56 an ATOM?
Yes
Is Y an ATOM?
Yes
Is 6 an ATOM?2
Yes
Is (MICE) a list?
Yes, because (MICE) is an ATOM enclosed in PARENTHESES
Is (MICE ARE NICE) a list?
Yes, because it is a collection of ATOMS enclosed in parentheses.

Is (MICE ARE) NICE a list?
No, because this is only two S-expressions not enclosed in parentheses. The first S-expression is a list and the second is an ATOM.
Is ((MICE ARE)NICE) a list?
Yes.
Is MICE and S-expression?
Yes, all ATOMS are S-expressions.
Is (MICE) an S-expression?
Yes, all lists are S-expressions.
Is the following a list: (IS THIS A LIST)
Yes, because it is a collection of S-expressions enclosed in parentheses.
Is the following example an S-expression: ((4)7)
Yes.
How many S-expressions are in this list?
(((MICE) ARE)((NICE)(TO EAT)(WITH RICE))
Three, they are:
((MICE) ARE), ((NICE) (TO EAT)) and ((WITH RICE).
Is the following a list: ()
Yes, it is the null list.
Is the following a list: (( ) ( ) ( ) ( ))
Yes.
What is the CAR of (A B C)?
A
What is the CAR of ((5 6)8 9)?
(5 6)
What is the CAR of MICE?
No answer, you can not ask the CAR of an ATOM.
What is the CAR of ( )
No answer, you can not ask the CAR of the null list.
What is the CDR of (7 8 9)?
(8 9)
What is the CDR of (A S(U I))?
(S(U I))
What is the CDR of ((W E R)Y U I)?
(Y U I)
What is the CDR of MICE?
You can not ask the CDR of an ATOM, therefore no answer.
What is the CDR of ( )?

No answer, you can not ask the CDR of the null list.
What is the CDR of (A)?
NIL
What is the CADR of ((T)(Y U)(H))?
(Y U)
What is the CAR of CDR called?
CADR
What is the CDR of CDR called?
CDDR
What is the CDR of CDR of CDR called?
CDDR
What is the CAR of CDR of CDR called?
CADDR

What is the value of (APPEND A B) if A is (7 8) and B is (5 6)?
(7 8 5 6)
What is the value of (APPEND A B) if A is (4 5 6) and B is (9)?
(4 5 6 9)
What is the value of (CONS A B) where A is (56) and B is (7 8)?
((56)7 8)
What is the value of (CONS A B) where A is (5 7) and B is ((4 6))?
((5 7)(4 6))
What is the value of (ATOM A) when A is 7?
T
What is the value of (ATOM A) when A is R (the symbol)?
T
What is the value of (ATOM A) when A is (5 6 7)?
NIL
What is the value of (NULL A) when A is 9
NIL
What is the value of (NULL A) when A is (6 7 8)?
NIL
What is the value of (NULL A) when A is NIL?
T
What is the value of (NULL(CDR A)) when A is (3)?
T
What is the value of (EQUAL A B) when A is (7) and B is (7)?

T

What is the value of (EQUAL A B) when A is (TIMES 4 5) and B is 20?
NIL

If A is 5 and B is (2 3 4 5 6) then (MEMBER A B) is?
T

If A is 7 and B is (8 5 9) then (MEMBER A B) is?
NIL

IF A is 3 and B is (4445) then (MEMBER A B) is?

What is the value of (OR T T)?
T

What is the value of (OR T NIL)?
T

What is the value of (OR NIL T) ?
T

What is the value of (OR NIL NIL)?
NIL

What is the value of (AND NIL T)?
NIL

What is the value of (AND T NIL)
NIL

What is the value of (AND NIL NIL)?
NIL

What is the value of (AND T T)?
T

What is the value of (NUMBERP A) when A is 6?
T

What is the value of (NUMBERP A) when A is T (the symbol)?
NIL

What is the value of (NUMBERP A) when A is (5 6 7)?
NIL

What is the value of (FIXP A) when A is when A is (5 6 7)?
NIL

What is the value of (FIXP A) when A is 8.9?
NIL

What is the value of (FIXP A) when A is 9?
T

What is the value of (FLOATP A) when A is 9?
NIL

What is the value of (FLOATP A) when A is 8.9?
T

If A is (5 6 89 9.8 67 5.9) what is the value of (COUNTFIXFLOAT A)?
(4 2)

If A is (TIMES 6 7) then (EVAL A) is?
42

If A is (LIST 678 5 89) then (EVAL A) is?
(678 5 89))

If A is (QUOTE MICE) then (EVAL A) is?
MICE

MORE LISP

What is missing?

Actually, almost all of LISP has been covered. There is still more, but as usual with different computer languages there is the problem of dialects. Each computer system might have a slightly different version of LISP, but rarely are the differences very significant. LISP is one of the few languages that is relatively standard from machine to machine. Even in standard versions, there are still some other points that should be covered.

What does the function RECIP do?

The function RECIP returns as its value the reciprocal of its argument. Therefore:

(RECIP 5) is 0.2
(RECIP 3) is 0. 333333
(RECIP 7) is 0.142857
(RECIP 2) is 0.5

What does the function FLOAT do?

The FLOAT function converts an integer number to a real number. A real number is a floating point number. This means that it can include decimals. Therefore:

(FLOAT 5) is 5.0
(FLOAT 67) is 67.0
(FLOAT 3) is 3.0
(FLOAT 100) is 100.0

What is the function ENTIER and what does it do?

The function ENTIER converts a floating point number to an integer.

Therefore:

(ENTIER 7.0) is 7
(ENTIER 6.0) is 6
(ENTIER 34.0) is 34
(ENTIER 78.0) is 78

What does EXPT do in LISP?
EXPT is the exponential function. Its value is the first argument raised to the power of the second argument. Therefore:
(EXPT 2 5) is 32
(EXPT 4 7) is 16384
(EXPT 3 8) is 6561
(EXPT 7 3) is 343

What is the MAX function?
The MAX (MAXIMUM) function consists of the function MAX plus a string of arguments. Its value is the largest or maximum value present in the string. Therefore:
(MAX 5 87 3 45 92) is 92
(MAX 654 34 2 897) is 897
(MAX 567 76 234 56) is 567
(MAX 1024 678 987) is 1024

What is the MIN function in LISP?
The MIN function is the inverse of the MAX function. Its value is that of the smallest or minimum value in its list. Therefore:
(MIN 56 4 78 43) is 4
(MIN 78 654 34) is 34
(MIN 567 1098 3456) is 567
(MIN 78 6 345 1) is 1

Are there increment and decrement functions in LISP?
Yes, they are ADD1 and SUB1. ADD1 dds one to its argument, while SUB1 subtracts one from its argument. This can be seen from the following examples:
(SUB1 45) is 44
(SUB1 23) is 22
(SUB 1 1025) is 1024
(SUB1 1) is 0
(ADD1 56) is 57
(ADD1 0) is 1
(ADD1 1067) is 1068
(ADD1 457) is 458

How can you determine if a number is even or odd?
Use the EVENP function which returns T if the argument is even and NIL if the argument is odd:
(EVENP 6) is T
(EVENP 77) is NIL
(EVENP 1024) is T
(EVENP 1023) is NIL

Can a function define another function in LISP and then use the function it has just defined?

Yes, this is usually done by using the DEFINE function at an inner level in the program or routine. In other words, the description of the given function (second argument of LAMBDA) can itself contain a DEFINE function.

If a particular routine or program has a considerable quantity of names in it, there can be serious problems. The LISP interpreter or compiler might become overloaded. There are many techniques that have evolved for solving this problem. You can pass the name of the internal function as a parameter:

(A B C D(QUOTE Q))

The function is A with the values (parameters B and C and D) which in the course of program execution will define an internal function with the name Q. Some LISP systems will use the word FUNCTION instead of the word QUOTE. And of course you can use the LAMBDA anywhere in the program.

What is the LABEL function in LISP?

The labelling function, called LABEL, has two arguments. The first argument is the name of a function, while the second argument is a description of the function so labelled. Quite typically the second argument will contain a LAMBDA expression.

What is the FUNCALL function?

The FUNCALL function enables function names or descriptions to be computed. Its first argument is used to calculate a function name or LAVBDA expression (description). Then it applies the resulting function to the rest of the argument—using as many as are needed for the function so defined in this way.

What else is important about QUOTE?

When LISP code is read from a terminal or from a file into the central memory the single quote marks (if they have been used) are translated into formal applications of the QUOTE function. This is necessary because the LISP interpreter requires all programs and data to be in the form of S-expressions.

What is the single quote mark?

The single quote mark is a replacement device for using " ' " instead of the word QUOTE and the accompanying parentheses. Therefore; 'S-expression equals (QUOTE S-expression).

LISP can be an interpreter but it also can be a compiler. How is that possible?

Most LISP systems are interpreters only. But they have a function called COMPILE.

What does this function do?
The LISP function COMPILE, allows the user to compile a LISP function. By compiling a function you can greatly increase execution speed. Compiling the function converts words into a series of instructions in the machine language of the computer.

Is the difference very significant between compile LISP and other compiled languages.
Yes, other languages require only that a certain portion of the language be present. For example, in FORTRAN the RUN-TIME module, which contains useful subroutines such as input—output routines, must be present. The LISP compiled object code requires the complete resources of the LISP system for subroutines. Therefore, the complete LISP system must remain in memory. The same occurs with WATFOR and WATFIV.

What is the function SPECIAL?
The SPECIAL function has only one argument. It is a list of variables (or the names of the variables) The function guarantees that the variables will retain its value from one usage of the program it is in to the next usage of the same program. This is somewhat like the OWN in ALGOL.

What is UNSPECIAL?
As the function name suggests, it is the reverse of SPECIAL. It declares that the variables in its argument are no longer to be considered special.

What is garbage collection in LISP?
The LISP system uses great amounts of memory to keep all the list pointers and circular lists. These are lists that are not S-expressions. They frequently have no right parenthesis, yet are quite useful. Garbage collection in LISP finds which words are available as free storage and collects them into a list. This allows the LISP system to run without filling all of the memory with lists that are no longer required. The garbage collection routine built into LISP must scan all the lists present in memory and determine which are no longer required.

ARTIFICIAL INTELLIGENCE

Artificial intelligence is the study of how to create computer programs that simulate the processes that seem to require human intelligent. AI programs are used in:

- Offices, to schedule the office work load, personnel draft documentation, prepare reports and use information that is on hand so that decisions can be formulated

- Farming and agriculture, the computer programs provide information for crop and pest control from the data sets.
- Manufacturing, by controlling equipment, there is less chance for error.
- Hospitals, programs have been designed to correlate symptoms with mental and physical problems.

Computers can also do intelligence tests. Programs have been devised that allow a computer to analyse a problem and arrive at the "correct" solution.

A computer program can "decide" that a "T" structure is a construction that requires one block to rest on the top of another block with the resting "block" exactly centered. This requires ideas about image detection and representation problem solving (Fig. 89).

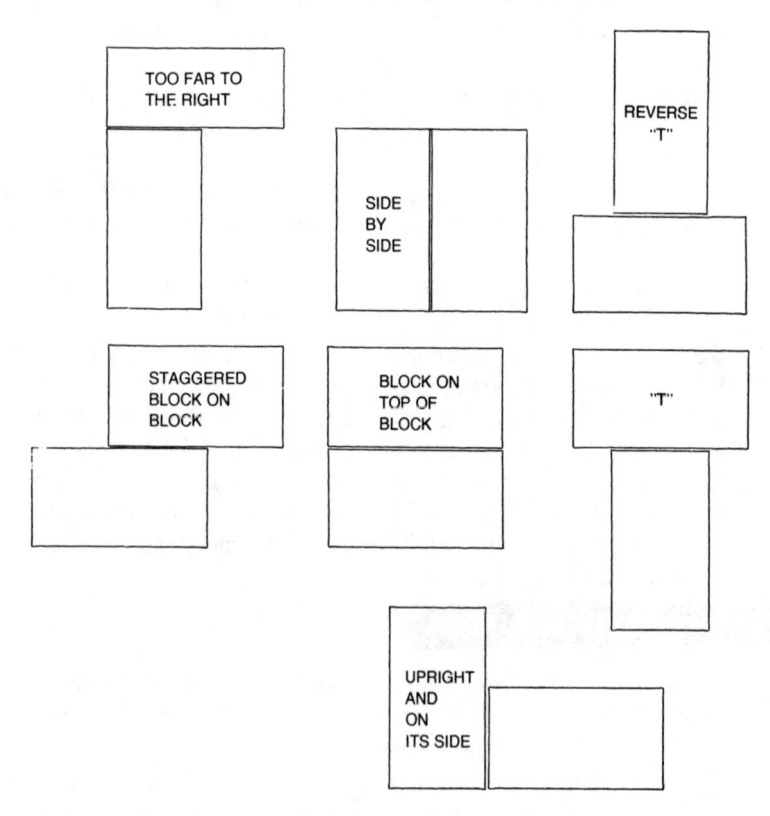

Fig. 89.

"Teaching" a computer program about the differences in lines, shadows and shading. A program can "view" a scene using a digitally encoded camera system and recognize the components therein (Fig. 90).

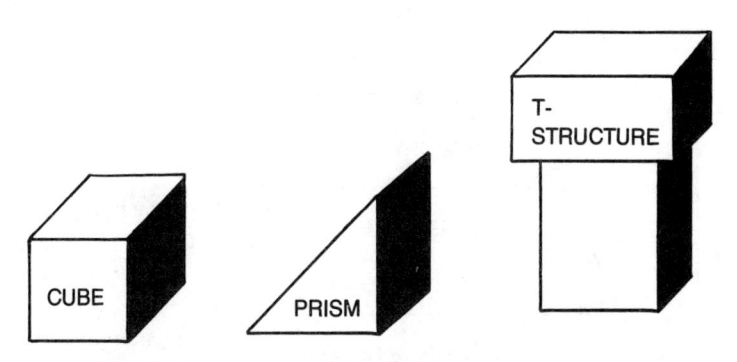

TYPICAL SCENES AS "VIEWED BY THE PROGRAM" ARE FILLED WITH SHADOWS, LINES, BOUNDARIES, CURVES AND CRACKS.

Fig. 90.

Programs can be designed that correlate data from mass spectrometers to determine the presence of different materials and elements. Error margin is considerably not require "human" intervention. It should be self-learning and modifying (Fig. 92). 1 : smaller with the "smart" machine (Fig. 91)

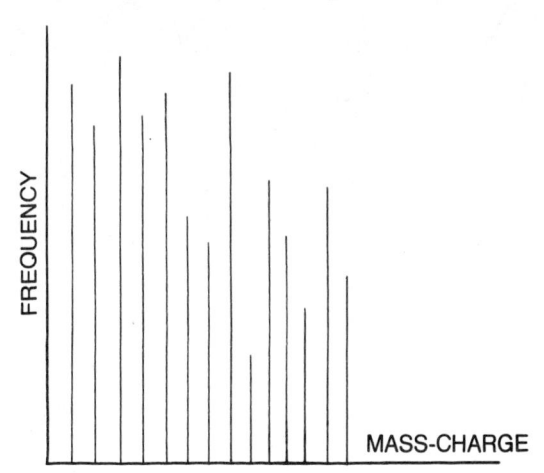

Fig. 91.

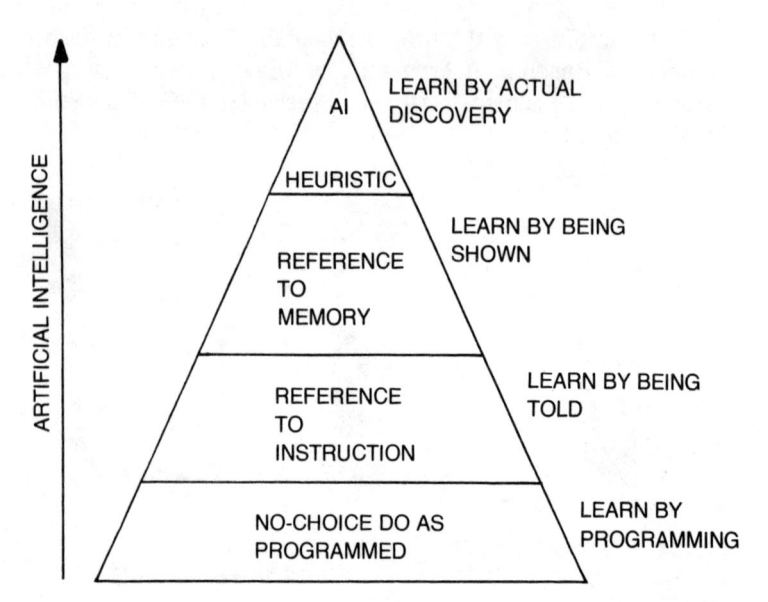

Fig. 92.

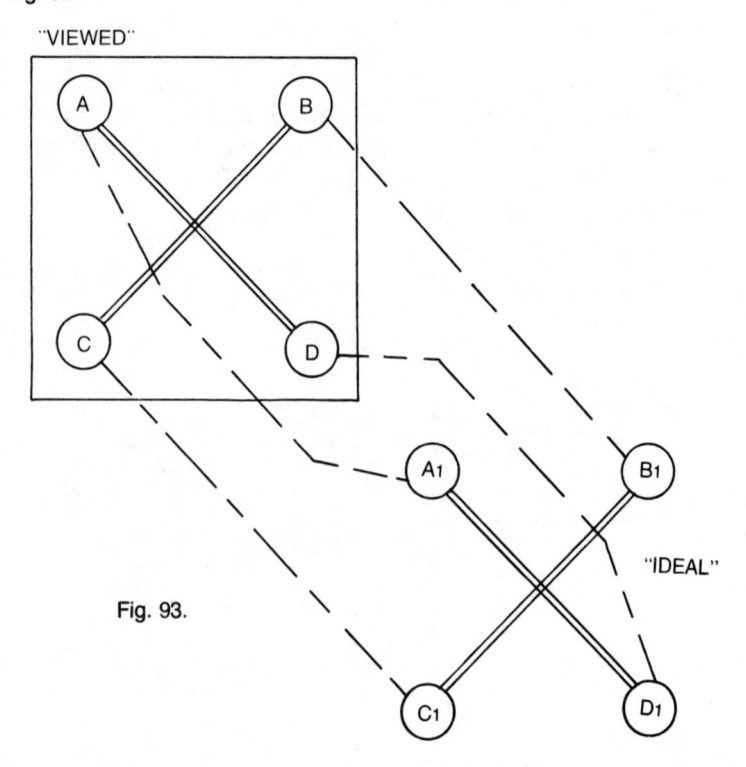

Fig. 93.

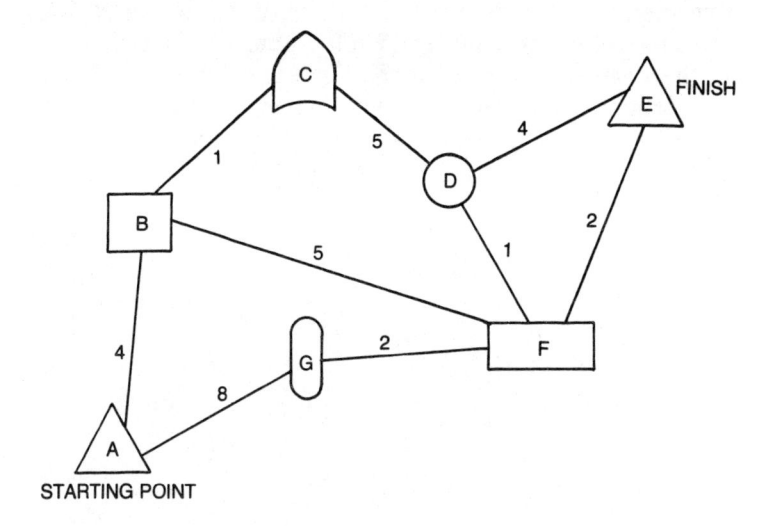

Fig. 94.

An artificial intelligence program does not require "human" intervention. It should be self-learning and modifying (Fig. 92).

A program can reference a set or sets of parameters to determine if the object being "viewed" is the desired object. This is accomplished by doing a one-to-one mapping of the parameters of the viewed object to that of the "ideal" object (Fig. 93).

A search problem requires the program to "pick" apart all the information given. The problem is to search or find the best route

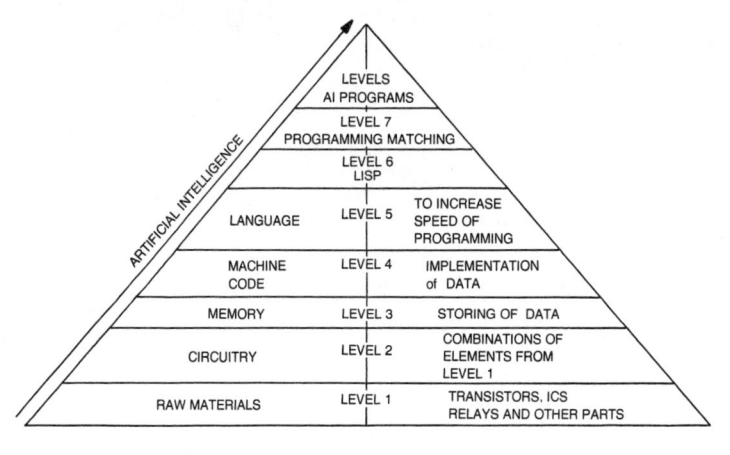

Fig. 95.

from point A to point E in terms of minimum distance traveled. The numbers reference distance units (relative units). It is obvious that the best path is A to B to F to E (Fig. 94).

Artificial intelligence programs, like any other highly sophisticated structures, depend on a strong and very large foundation (Fig. 95).

Part Two: Programs and Examples

The following section contains programs and examples written in LISP. It should be noted that in certain routines the LAMBDA function was not used. Certain LISP systems allow a definition to be carried out without resorting to LAMBDA. In this case, the arguments of the function being defined are enclosed within the same parentheses with the function name.

ADD

Requirement

To be able to use a LIST as a DATA-BASE and ADD information to this DATA-BASE. DATA is the name of the LIST and I is the new information.

Program

```
(DEFINE
(ADD I)
(COND(( MEMBER
I DATA)
NIL)
(T
(SETQ DATA
(CONS I DATA))
I)))
```

Notice that this routine checks whether the new information I is already present in the list before it adds it. The function will return NIL if the information is already present or it will return the information (I) if it is not present and the routine has added it to the "DATA-BASE."

Sample Run

Assume the LIST is MICE RAT LION.
(ADD I) where I is the ATOM MOUSE
MOUSE

(ADD I) where I is the ATOM MICE
NIL

(ADD I) where I is the ATOM CAT
CAT
(ADD I) where I is RAT
NIL

END

Flowchart: Add

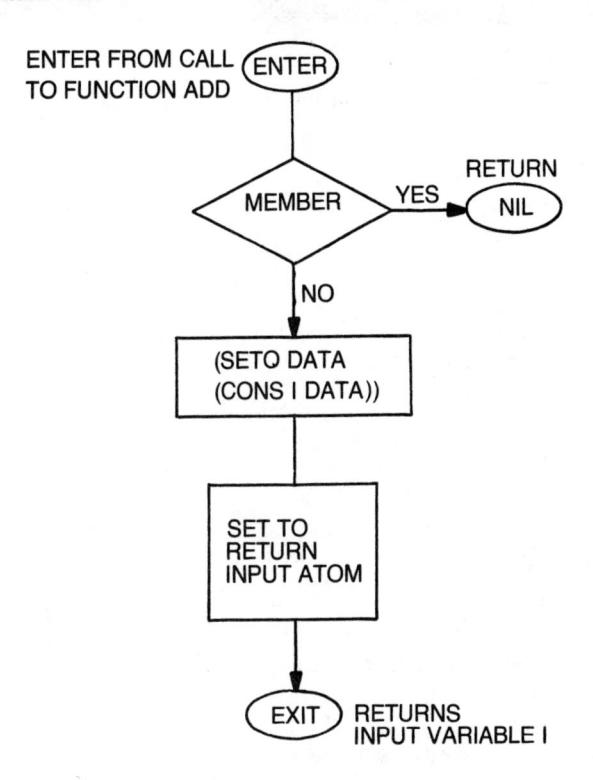

ENTER FROM CALL TO FUNCTION ADD → (ENTER)

MEMBER — YES → RETURN (NIL)

NO ↓

(SETQ DATA
(CONS I DATA))

↓

SET TO
RETURN
INPUT ATOM

↓

(EXIT) RETURNS INPUT VARIABLE I

ANNULAR MOMENT OF INERTIA

Requirement

To find the moment of inertia of an annulus.

Program

```
(DEFINE
(AMI D1 D2)
(QUOTIENT
(TIMES
(DIFFERENCE
(EXPT D2 4)
(EXPT D1 4))
3.14159
64)
)
```

Sample Run

```
(AMI 1 2)
0.7363
```
****
```
(AMI 3 4)
8.590
```
****
```
(AMI 5 6)
32.93
```
****
```
(AMI 7 8)
83.20
```
****
END

Flowchart: Annular Moment of Inertia

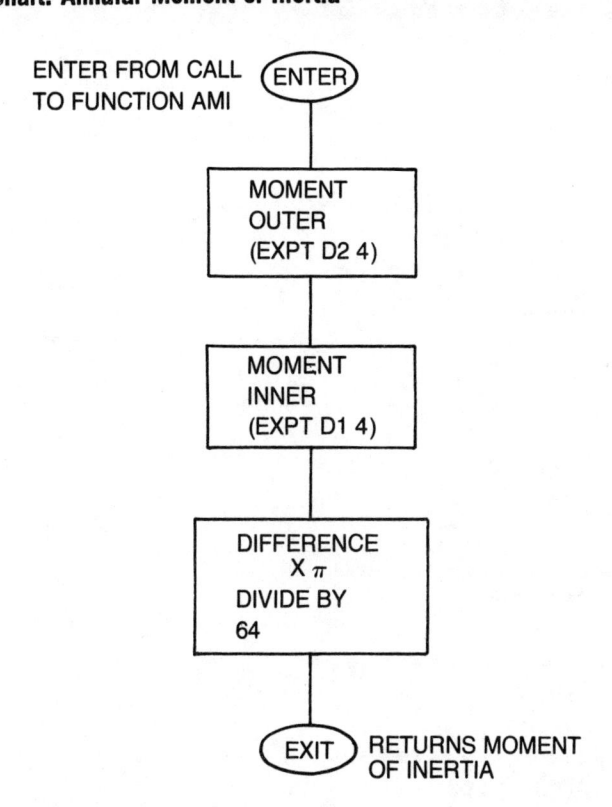

ENTER FROM CALL TO FUNCTION AMI → (ENTER)

- MOMENT OUTER (EXPT D2 4)
- MOMENT INNER (EXPT D1 4)
- DIFFERENCE X π DIVIDE BY 64

(EXIT) RETURNS MOMENT OF INERTIA

ANNULAR POLAR MOMENT

Program
```
(DEFINE
(APM D2 D1)
(QUOTIENT
(TIMES
(DIFFERENCE
(TIMES D2 D2 D2 D2)
(TIMES D1 D1 D1 D1))
3.14159
32)
)
```

Sample Run
```
(APM 2 1)
1.4726
```
****
```
(APM 4 3)
17.1806
```
****
```
(APM 8 7)
166.406
```
****
```
(APM 10 9)
337.623
```
****
END

Flowchart: Annular Polar Moment

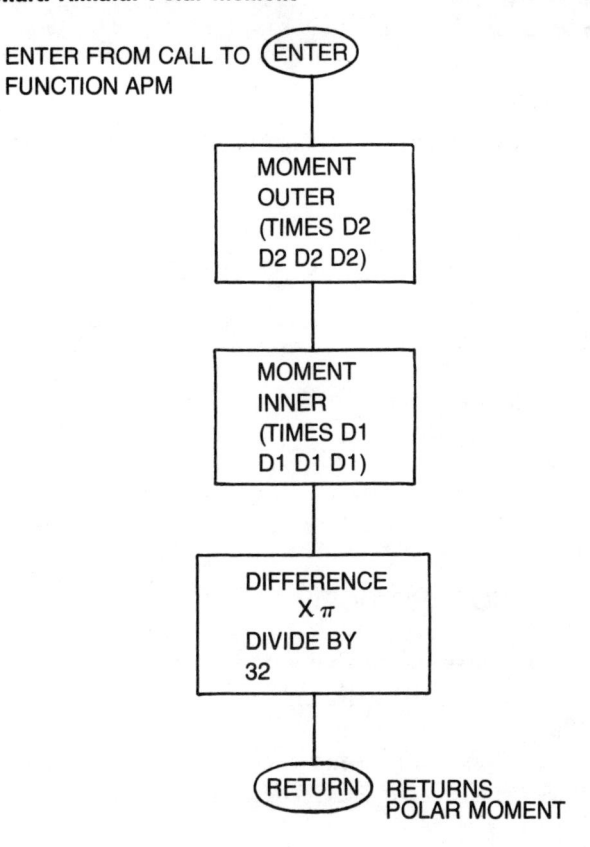

ENTER FROM CALL TO (ENTER)
FUNCTION APM

- MOMENT OUTER (TIMES D2 D2 D2 D2)
- MOMENT INNER (TIMES D1 D1 D1 D1)
- DIFFERENCE X π DIVIDE BY 32

(RETURN) RETURNS POLAR MOMENT

ATOM CHECK

Requirement
To check to see if a list contains only ATOMS and no sub-lists.

Program
```
(DEFINE
(LIS L)
(COND
((NULL L)
T)
((AOM(CAR L))
(LIS (CDR L)))
(T NIL)
)))))
```

Sample Run
```
(LIS '(MICE ARE NICE))
T
```
****
```
(LIS '(MICE (ARE) NICE))
NIL
```
****
```
(LIS '(IS THIS (A) GOOD TEST))
NIL
```
****
```
(LIS '(ARE ELEPHANTS ALWAYS HUNGRY))
T
```
****
```
(LIS '( ))
T
```
****
```
(LIS '((MICE) ARE (GOOD) WITH (RICE))
NIL
```
****
```
END
```

Flowchart: Atom Check

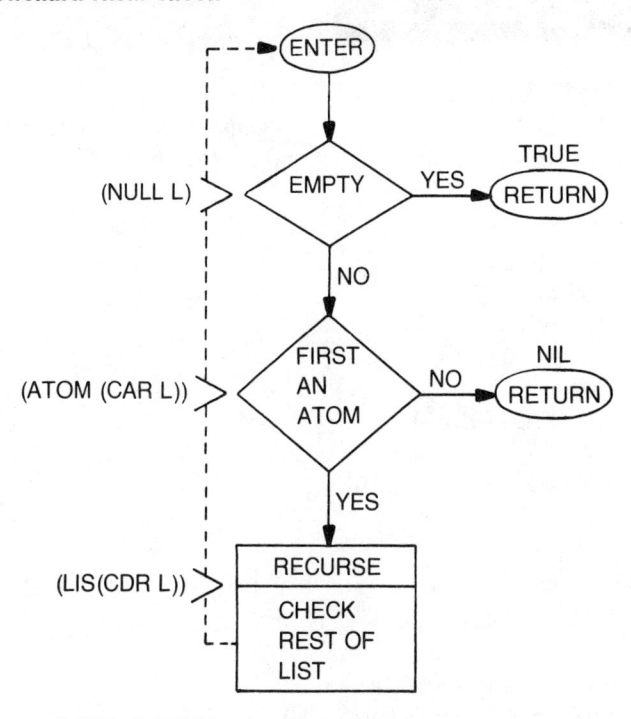

(NULL L) — EMPTY — YES → TRUE RETURN

NO ↓

(ATOM (CAR L)) — FIRST AN ATOM — NO → NIL RETURN

YES ↓

(LIS(CDR L)) — RECURSE / CHECK REST OF LIST

(NOTE: DOTTED LINE REFERS TO RECURSION PATH)

ATOM MEMBER OF A LIST

Requirement
To check whether the first argument is a member of the second argument which is a list and the first is an ATOM.

Program
```
(DEFINE
(MEM A L)
(COND
((NULL L)
NIL)
((EQ (CAR L) A)
T)
(T (MEM A (CDR L)))
))
```

Sample Run
```
(MEM'ARE'(MICE ARE NICE))
T
********************
(MEM'HOUSE' ? ())|    NIL
********************
(MEM'A'(G Y E A D Y))
T
********************
(MEM'F'(I J U F O))
T
********************
(MEM'RED'(PINK GREEN ORANGE))
NIL
********************
END
```

Flowchart: Atom Member of a List

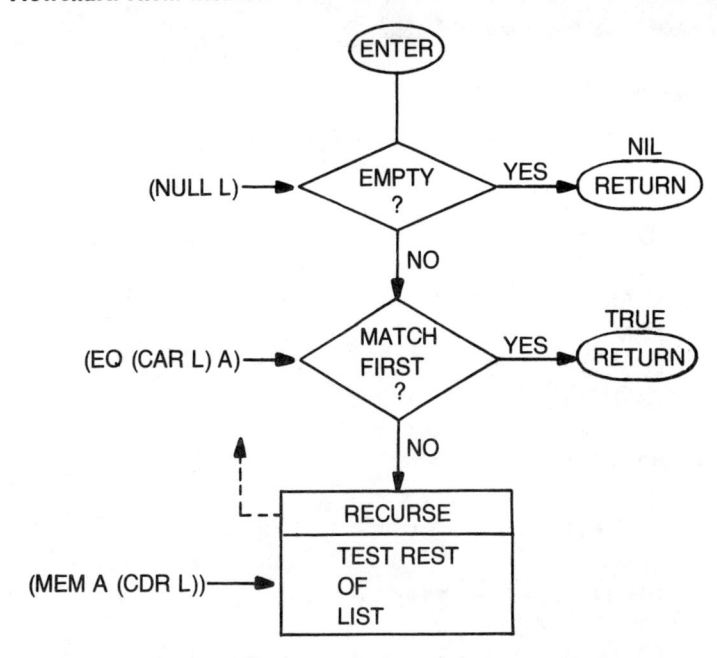

```
                        ENTER
                          │
                          ▼
                      ┌─────────┐    YES      NIL
        (NULL L) ──▶  │ EMPTY ? │ ──────▶  RETURN
                      └─────────┘
                          │ NO
                          ▼
                      ┌─────────┐    YES     TRUE
    (EQ (CAR L) A)──▶ │  MATCH  │ ──────▶  RETURN
                      │  FIRST? │
                      └─────────┘
                          │ NO
              ┌───────────▼────────────┐
              │       RECURSE          │
              ├────────────────────────┤
   (MEM A (CDR L)) ──▶ TEST REST       │
              │         OF             │
              │         LIST           │
              └────────────────────────┘
```

NOTE: RECURSION RETURNS TO THE INITIAL POINT OF CALL OF THE ROUTINE WITH NEW VARIABLE(S). THE DOTTED LINE REFERS TO RECURSION PATH.

CIRCULAR POLAR MOMENT

Requirement
To find the polar moment of inertia of a circle.

Program
```
(DEFINE
(CPM D)
(TIMES
(TIMES D
(TIMES D D D))
.098175)
```

Sample Run
```
(SETQ D 1)
(CPM D)
.098175
```
****
```
(SETQ D 2)
(CPM D)
1.5708
```
****
```
(CPM 3)
7.95215
```
****
```
(CPM 4)
25.133
```
****
```
END
```

Flowchart: Circular Polar Moment

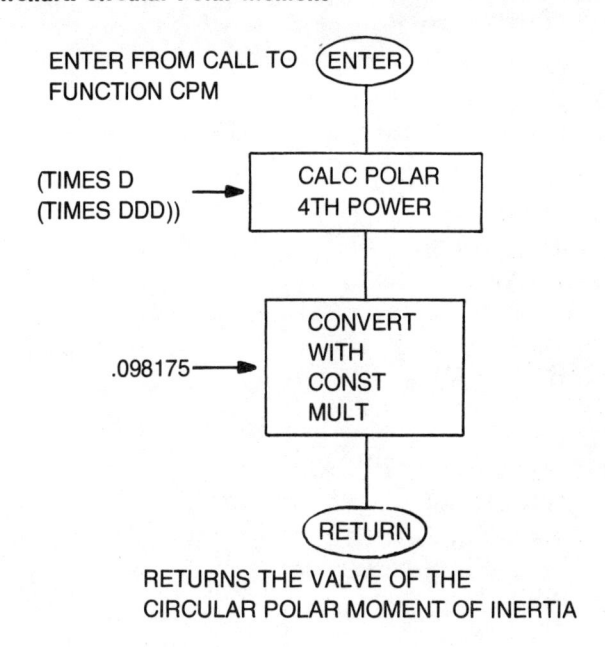

ENTER FROM CALL TO (ENTER)
FUNCTION CPM

(TIMES D → CALC POLAR
(TIMES DDD)) 4TH POWER

.098175 → CONVERT
WITH
CONST
MULT

(RETURN)

RETURNS THE VALVE OF THE
CIRCULAR POLAR MOMENT OF INERTIA

133

COMPLEX ADDITION

Requirement

To find the sum of two complex numbers.

Program

```
(DEFINE
(COMPLUS A B)
(SETQ A1
(CAR A))
(SETQ A
(CAR (CDR A)))
(SETQ B1
(CAR B))
(SETQ B2
(CAR (CDR B)))
(SETQ X (PLUS A1 B1))
(SETQ Y (PLUS A2 B2))
(CONS X
(CONS Y NIL))
)
```

Sample Run

```
(COMPLUS '(1 0) '(2 0))
(3 0)
********************
(COMPLUS '(1 2) '(3 4))
(4 6)
********************
END
```

Flowchart: Complex Addition

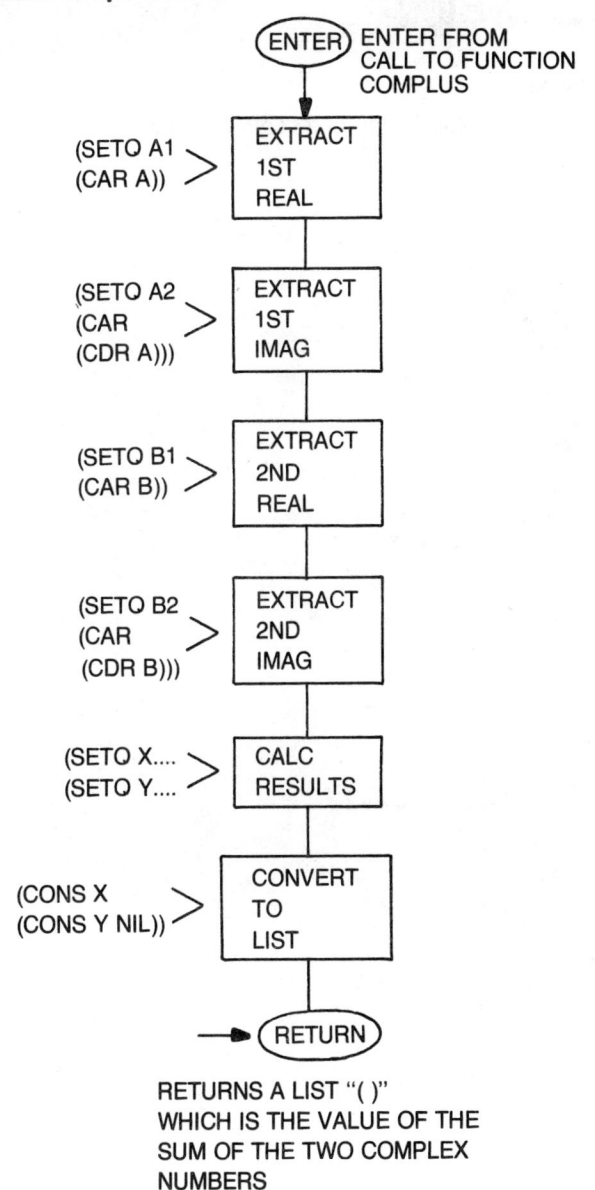

```
                          ┌─────────┐  ENTER FROM
                         ( ENTER  )  CALL TO FUNCTION
                          └────┬────┘  COMPLUS
                               ▼
    (SETO A1           ┌─────────────┐
     (CAR A))    ────▶ │  EXTRACT    │
                       │  1ST        │
                       │  REAL       │
                       └──────┬──────┘
                              ▼
    (SETO A2           ┌─────────────┐
     (CAR         ────▶│  EXTRACT    │
      (CDR A)))        │  1ST        │
                       │  IMAG       │
                       └──────┬──────┘
                              ▼
    (SETO B1           ┌─────────────┐
     (CAR B))    ────▶ │  EXTRACT    │
                       │  2ND        │
                       │  REAL       │
                       └──────┬──────┘
                              ▼
    (SETO B2           ┌─────────────┐
     (CAR         ────▶│  EXTRACT    │
      (CDR B)))        │  2ND        │
                       │  IMAG       │
                       └──────┬──────┘
                              ▼
    (SETO X....        ┌─────────────┐
     (SETO Y....  ────▶│  CALC       │
                       │  RESULTS    │
                       └──────┬──────┘
                              ▼
    (CONS X            ┌─────────────┐
     (CONS Y NIL))────▶│  CONVERT    │
                       │  TO         │
                       │  LIST       │
                       └──────┬──────┘
                              ▼
                         ┌─────────┐
                    ────▶( RETURN  )
                         └─────────┘
```

RETURNS A LIST "( )"
WHICH IS THE VALUE OF THE
SUM OF THE TWO COMPLEX
NUMBERS

COMPLEX CONJUGATE

Requirement

to find the absolute value of a complex number.

Program
```
(DEFINE
(CCON A)
(SETQ A1)
(CAR A))
(SETQ A2
(CAR
(CDR A)))
EXPT
(PLUS
(TIMES A1 A1)
(TIMES A2 A2)).5)
```

Sample Run
```
(CCON '(1 0))
1
********************
(CCON '(1 1))
1.414
********************
(CCON '(2 3))
3.605
********************
(CCON '(4 5))
6.403
********************
END
```

136

Flowchart: Complex Conjugate

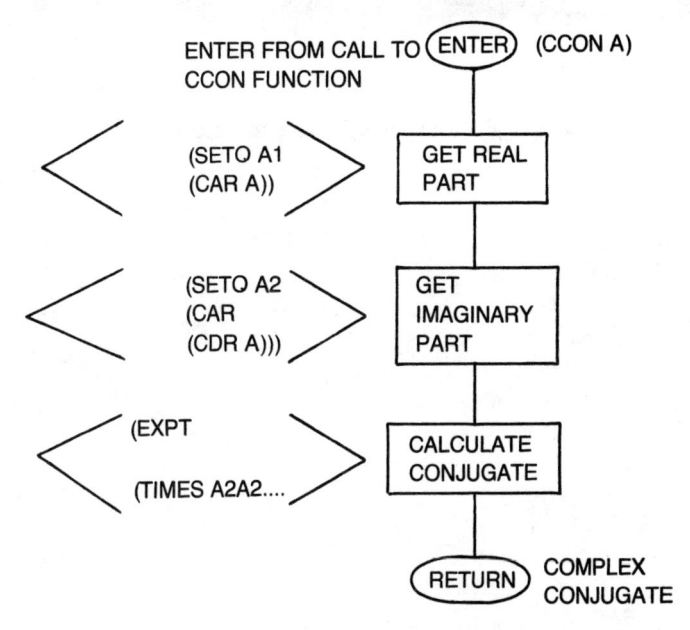

ENTER FROM CALL TO (ENTER) (CCON A)
CCON FUNCTION

- (SETQ A1 (CAR A)) → **GET REAL PART**
- (SETQ A2 (CAR (CDR A))) → **GET IMAGINARY PART**
- (EXPT (TIMES A2 A2 .... → **CALCULATE CONJUGATE**

(RETURN) COMPLEX CONJUGATE

RETURNS THE ABSOLUTE VALUE OF THE ENTERED COMPLEX NUMBER

137

COMPLEX DIVISION

Requirement

to find the quotient of two complex numbers.

Program

```
(DEFINE
(COMQUO A B)
(SETQ A1
(CAR A))
(SETQ A2)
(CAR
(CDR A)))
(SETQ B1
(CAR B))
(SETQ B2
(CAR
(CDR B)))
(SETQ X
(QUOTIENT
(PLUS
(TIMES A1 A2)
(TIMES B1 B2))
(PLUS
(TIMES A2 A2)
(TIMES B2 B2))))
(SETQ Y
(QUOTIENT
(DIFFERENCE
(TIMES A2 B1)
(TIMES A1 B2))
(PLUS
(TIMES A2 A2)
(TIMES B2 B2))))
(CONS X
(CONS Y NIL))
)
```

Sample Run

```
(COMQUO '(2 0) '(1 0))
(2 0)
```

```
********************

    (COMQUO '(1 1) '(2 1))
    ( .6 .2)
********************

    (COMQUO '(12 15) '(27 32))
    (.46 .11)
********************
    END
```

Flowchart: Complex Division

FLOWCHART: COMPLEX DIVISION

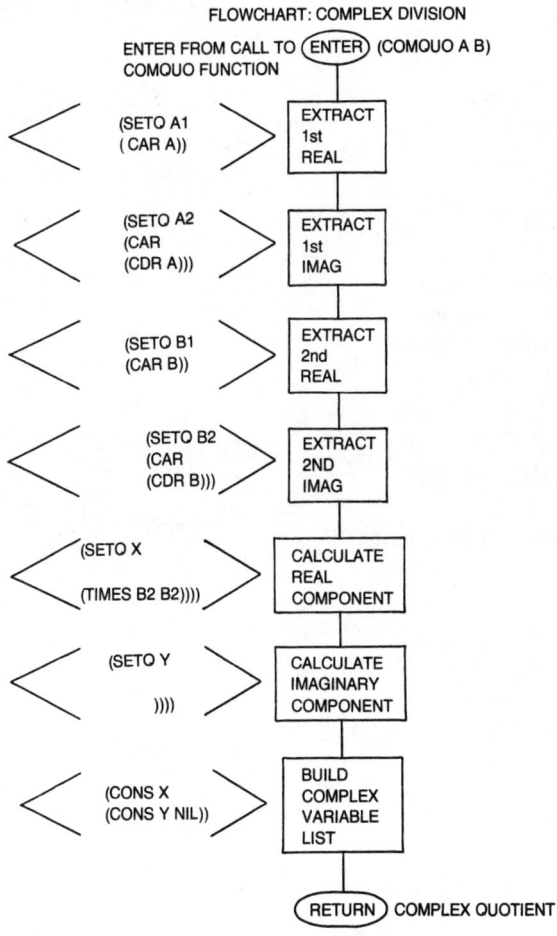

ENTER FROM CALL TO COMQUO FUNCTION → (ENTER) (COMQUO A B)

- (SETQ A1 (CAR A)) → **EXTRACT 1st REAL**
- (SETQ A2 (CAR (CDR A))) → **EXTRACT 1st IMAG**
- (SETQ B1 (CAR B)) → **EXTRACT 2nd REAL**
- (SETQ B2 (CAR (CDR B))) → **EXTRACT 2ND IMAG**
- (SETQ X (TIMES B2 B2)))) → **CALCULATE REAL COMPONENT**
- (SETQ Y)))) → **CALCULATE IMAGINARY COMPONENT**
- (CONS X (CONS Y NIL)) → **BUILD COMPLEX VARIABLE LIST**

(RETURN) COMPLEX QUOTIENT

RETURNS A LIST "( )" CONTAINING THE QUOTIENT OF THE TWO COMPLEX NUMBERS

COMPLEX MULTIPLICATION

Requirement
To find the product of two complex numbers.

Program
```
(DEFINE
(COMTIMES A B)
(SETQ A1
(CAR A))
(SETQ A2
(CAR
(CDR A)))
(SETQ B1
(CAR B))
(SETQ B2
(CAR
(CDR B)))
(SETQ X
(DIFFERENCE
(TIMES A1 A2)
(TIMES B1 B2)))
(SETQ Y
(PLUS
(TIMES A1 B2)
(TIMES A2 B1)))
(CONS X
(CONS Y NIL))
)
```

Sample Run
```
(SETQ A '(1 0))
(SETQ B '(2 0))
(COMTIMES A B)
(2 0)
```
****
```
(SETQ A '(1 1))
(SETQ B '(2 1))
(COMTIMES A B)
(1 3)
```
****

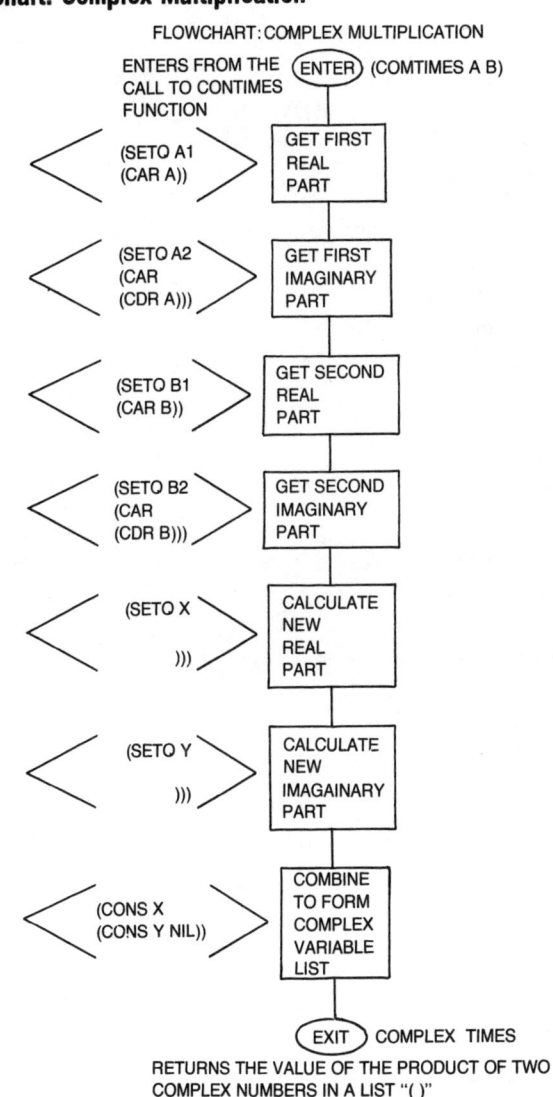

```
(COMTIMES'(1 1)'(4 7))
(-3 11)
```
****
```
(COMTIMES '(12 15) '(27 32))
(-156 789)
```
****
END

Flowchart: Complex Multiplication

FLOWCHART: COMPLEX MULTIPLICATION

ENTERS FROM THE CALL TO CONTIMES FUNCTION → (ENTER) (COMTIMES A B)

(SETQ A1 (CAR A)) — GET FIRST REAL PART

(SETQ A2 (CAR (CDR A))) — GET FIRST IMAGINARY PART

(SETQ B1 (CAR B)) — GET SECOND REAL PART

(SETQ B2 (CAR (CDR B))) — GET SECOND IMAGINARY PART

(SETQ X))) — CALCULATE NEW REAL PART

(SETQ Y))) — CALCULATE NEW IMAGINARY PART

(CONS X (CONS Y NIL)) — COMBINE TO FORM COMPLEX VARIABLE LIST

(EXIT) COMPLEX TIMES

RETURNS THE VALUE OF THE PRODUCT OF TWO COMPLEX NUMBERS IN A LIST "( )"

COMPLEX RECIPROCAL

Requirement
to find the reciprocal of a complex number.

Program
```
(DEFINE
(CREC A)
(SETQ A1 (CAR A))
(SETQ A2 (CAR (CDR A)))
(SETQ X (QUOTIENT A1 (PLUS
(TIMES A1 A1)
(TIMES B1 B1))))
(SETQ Y (QUOTIENT (MINUS B1)
(PLUS
(TIMES A1 A1)
(TIMES B1 B1))))
(CONS X (CONS Y NIL))
)
```

Sample Run
```
(CREC '(1 0))
(1 0)
```
****
```
(CREC '(1 1))
( .5 -.5)
```
****
```
(CREC '(2 3))
(.15 -.23)
```
****
END

Flowchart: Complex Reciprocal

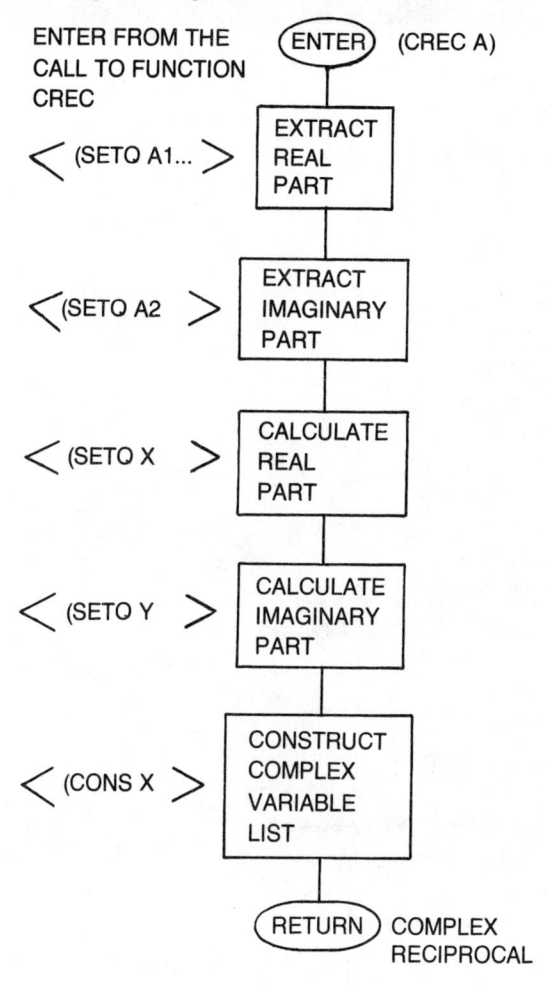

ENTER FROM THE CALL TO FUNCTION CREC

(ENTER) (CREC A)

(SETQ A1...) → EXTRACT REAL PART

(SETQ A2) → EXTRACT IMAGINARY PART

(SETQ X) → CALCULATE REAL PART

(SETQ Y) → CALCULATE IMAGINARY PART

(CONS X) → CONSTRUCT COMPLEX VARIABLE LIST

(RETURN) COMPLEX RECIPROCAL

RETURNS THE COMPLEX RECIPROCAL OF THE ENTERED COMPLEX NUMBER

143

COMPLEX SUBTRACTION

Requirement
```
(DEFINE
(CSUB A B)
(SETQ A1)
(CAR A))
SETQ B1
(CAR B))
(SETQ B2
(CAR
(CDR B)))
(SETQ A2
CAR
(CDR A)))
(SETQ X
(DIFFERENCE A1 B1 ))
(SETQ Y
(DIFFERENCE A2 B2))
(CONS X (CONS Y NIL))
)
```

Sample Run
```
(CSUB '(1 0) '(1 0))
(0 0)
```
****
```
(CSUB '(2 1) '(1 0))
(1 1)
```
****
```
END
```

Flowchart: Complex Subtraction

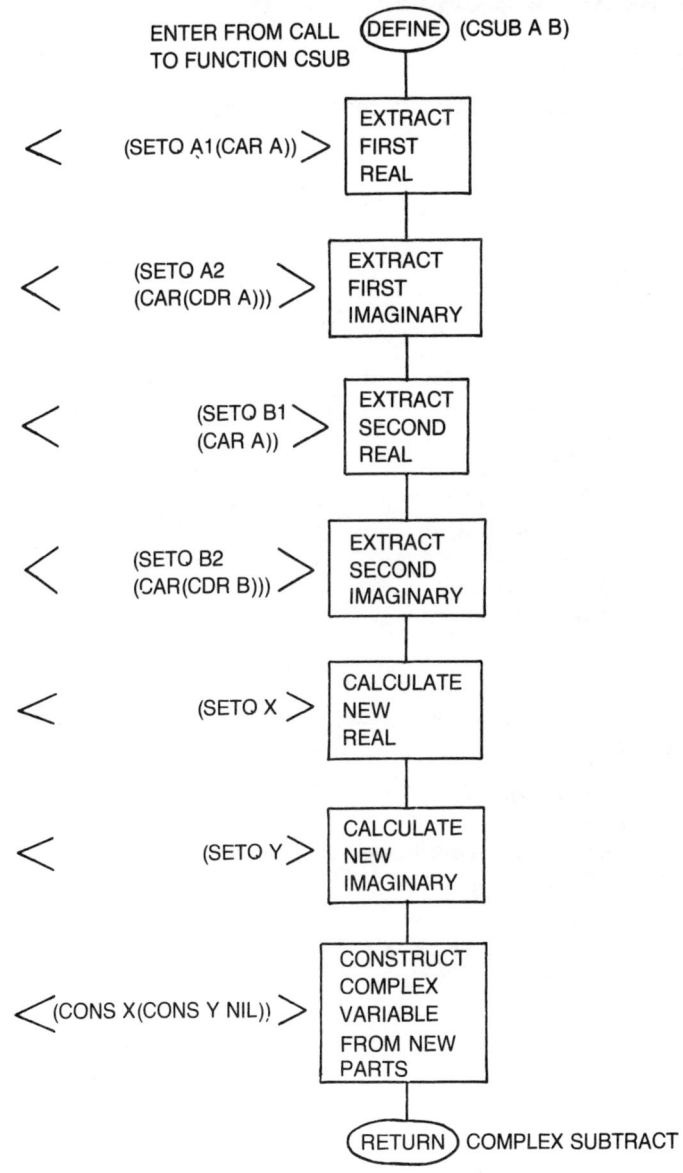

ENTER FROM CALL TO FUNCTION CSUB → (DEFINE) (CSUB A B)

- (SETO A1 (CAR A)) → **EXTRACT FIRST REAL**
- (SETO A2 (CAR (CDR A))) → **EXTRACT FIRST IMAGINARY**
- (SETO B1 (CAR A)) → **EXTRACT SECOND REAL**
- (SETO B2 (CAR (CDR B))) → **EXTRACT SECOND IMAGINARY**
- (SETO X) → **CALCULATE NEW REAL**
- (SETO Y) → **CALCULATE NEW IMAGINARY**
- (CONS X (CONS Y NIL)) → **CONSTRUCT COMPLEX VARIABLE FROM NEW PARTS**

(RETURN) COMPLEX SUBTRACT

RETURNS A LIST "( )" CONTAINING THE REMAINDER PRODUCED BY SUBTRACTING TWO COMPLEX NUMBERS.

COMPLEX SQUARE

Requirement
To find the square of a complex number.

Program
```
(DEFINE
(CSR A)
(SETQ A1)
(CAR A))
(SETQ A2
(CAR
(CDR A)))
(SETQ X
(DIFFERENCE
(TIMES A1 A1)
(TIMES A2 A2)))
(SETQ Y
(TIMES 2 A1 A2))
(CONS X
(CONS Y NIL))
)
```

Sample Run
```
(CSR '(1 0))
(1 0)
```
****
```
(CSR '(! '(1 2))
(-3 4)
```
****
END

Flowchart: Complex Square

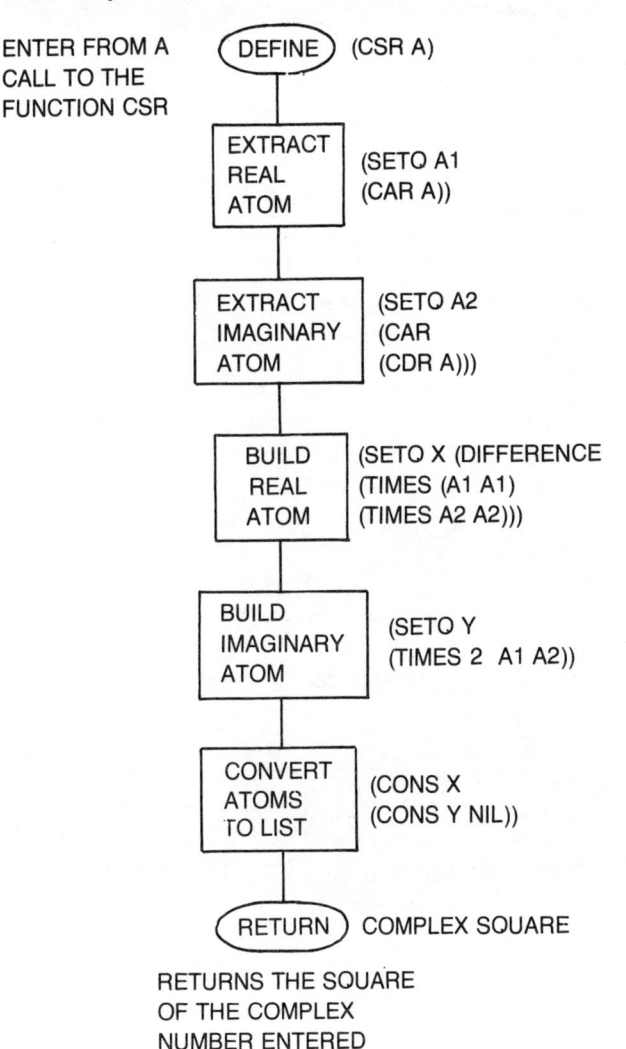

ENTER FROM A CALL TO THE FUNCTION CSR

(DEFINE) (CSR A)

| EXTRACT REAL ATOM | (SETQ A1 (CAR A)) |

| EXTRACT IMAGINARY ATOM | (SETQ A2 (CAR (CDR A))) |

| BUILD REAL ATOM | (SETQ X (DIFFERENCE (TIMES A1 A1) (TIMES A2 A2))) |

| BUILD IMAGINARY ATOM | (SETQ Y (TIMES 2 A1 A2)) |

| CONVERT ATOMS TO LIST | (CONS X (CONS Y NIL)) |

(RETURN) COMPLEX SQUARE

RETURNS THE SQUARE OF THE COMPLEX NUMBER ENTERED

COMPLEX SQUARE ROOT

Requirement

To find the square root of a complex number.

Program

```
(DEFINE
(CSQRT A)
(SETQ A1 (CAR A))
(SETQ A2 (CAR (CDR A)))
(SETQ X
(EXPT
(QUOTIENT
(PLUS A1
(EXPT
(PLUS
(TIMES A1 A1)
(TIMES A2 A2))
.5))
2)
.5))
(SETQ Y (QUOTIENT A2
(TIMES 2
(EXPT
(QUOTIENT (EXPT
(PLUS
(TIMES A1 A1)
(TIMES A2 A2)).5)2).5))))
(CONS X (CONS Y NIL))
)
```

Sample Run

```
(CSQRT '(1 0))
(1 0)
```
****
```
(CSQRT '(1 1))
(1.09 .45)
```
****
```
(CSQRT '(1 2))
(1.27 .78)
```
****

```
(CSQRT '(3 4))
(2 1)
*********************
   END
```

Flowchart: Complex Square Root

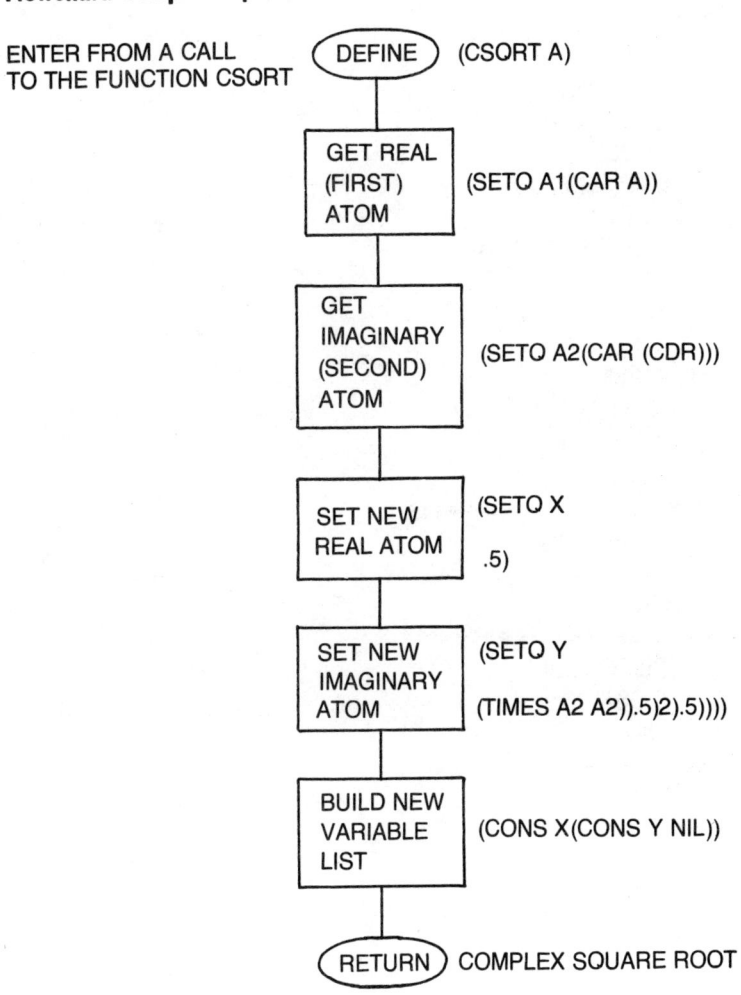

ENTER FROM A CALL TO THE FUNCTION CSQRT → (DEFINE) (CSQRT A)

| GET REAL (FIRST) ATOM | (SETQ A1(CAR A)) |

| GET IMAGINARY (SECOND) ATOM | (SETQ A2(CAR (CDR))) |

| SET NEW REAL ATOM | (SETQ X .5) |

| SET NEW IMAGINARY ATOM | (SETQ Y (TIMES A2 A2)).5)2).5)))) |

| BUILD NEW VARIABLE LIST | (CONS X(CONS Y NIL)) |

(RETURN) COMPLEX SQUARE ROOT

RETURNS A LIST "( )" CONTAINING THE SQUARE ROOT OF THE ENTERED COMPLEX NUMBER

COSH (X)

Requirement
To find the value of COSH(X).

Program
```
(DEFINE
(COSH X)
(QUOTIENT
(PLUS
(EXPT 2.718 X)
(RECIP
(EXPT 2.718 X)))
2)
)
```

Sample Run
```
(SETQ X 1)
(COSH X)
1.543
```
****
```
(SETQ X 2)
(COSH X)
3.762
```
****
```
(SETQ X 3I
(COSH X)
10.07
```
****
END

Flowchart: COSH(X)

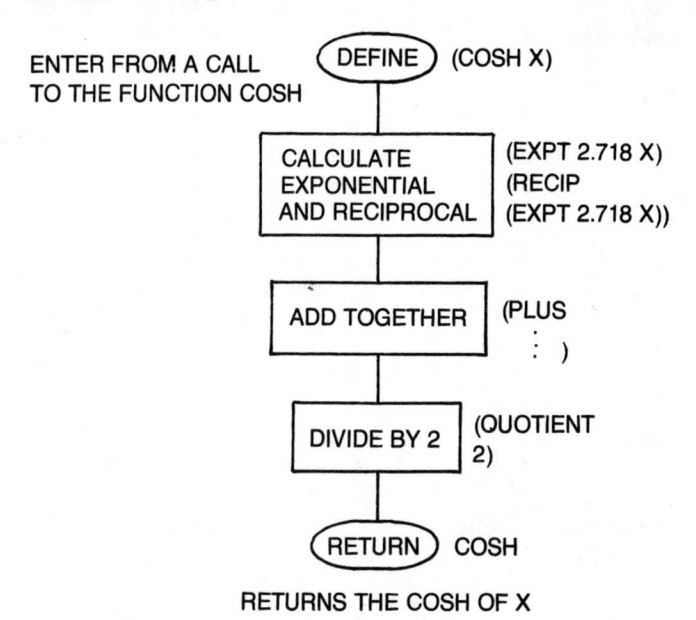

ENTER FROM A CALL TO THE FUNCTION COSH

(DEFINE) (COSH X)

CALCULATE EXPONENTIAL AND RECIPROCAL — (EXPT 2.718 X) (RECIP (EXPT 2.718 X))

ADD TOGETHER — (PLUS
⋮
⋮)

DIVIDE BY 2 — (QUOTIENT
2)

(RETURN) COSH

RETURNS THE COSH OF X

COTH (X)

Requirement
To find the value of COTH(X).

Program
```
(DEFINE
(COTH X)
(QUOTIENT
(PLUS
(EXPT 2.718
(MINUS X)))
(DIFFERENCE
(EXPT 2.718 X)
(RECIP
(EXPT 2.718 X))))
)
```

Sample Run
```
(COTH 1)
1.313
********************
(COTH 2)
1.037
********************
(COTH 5)
1.000
********************
END
```

Flowchart: COTH (X)

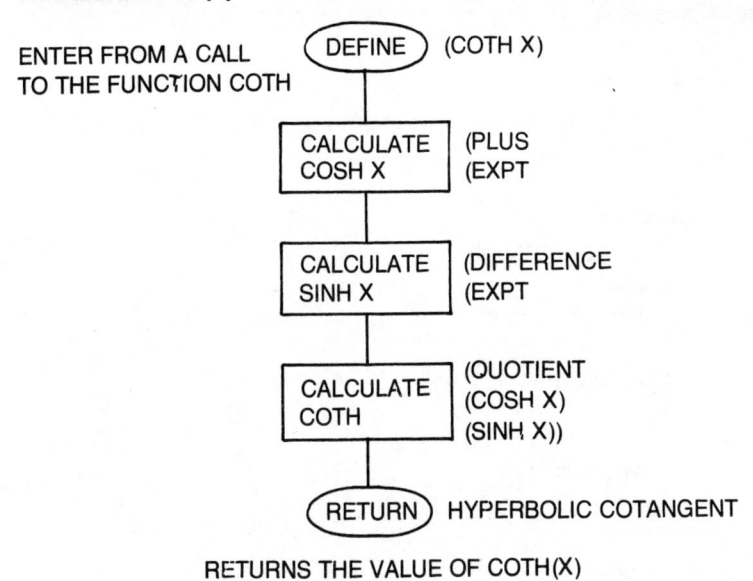

ENTER FROM A CALL
TO THE FUNCTION COTH

(DEFINE) (COTH X)

CALCULATE COSH X	(PLUS (EXPT
CALCULATE SINH X	(DIFFERENCE (EXPT
CALCULATE COTH	(QUOTIENT (COSH X) (SINH X))

(RETURN) HYPERBOLIC COTANGENT

RETURNS THE VALUE OF COTH(X)

COUNT

Requirement

To count the number of ATOMS in an S-expression where X is the S-expression.

Program

```
(DEFINE (CTA X)
(COND
((NULL X)
0)
((ATOM X)
1)
(T
(APPLY 'PLUS
(MAPCAR 'CTA X)))))
```

Sample Run

```
You must set X to the list desired.
(SETQ X (QUOTE (MICE ARE NICE)))
(CTA X)
3
********************
(SETQ X '(MINUTES IN THE HOUR))
(CTA X)
4
********************
(SETQ X '(HOW ARE YOU TODAY ALEC))
(CTA X)
5
********************
(SETQ X (QUOTE MICE))
(CTA X)
1
********************
END
```

Flowchart: Count

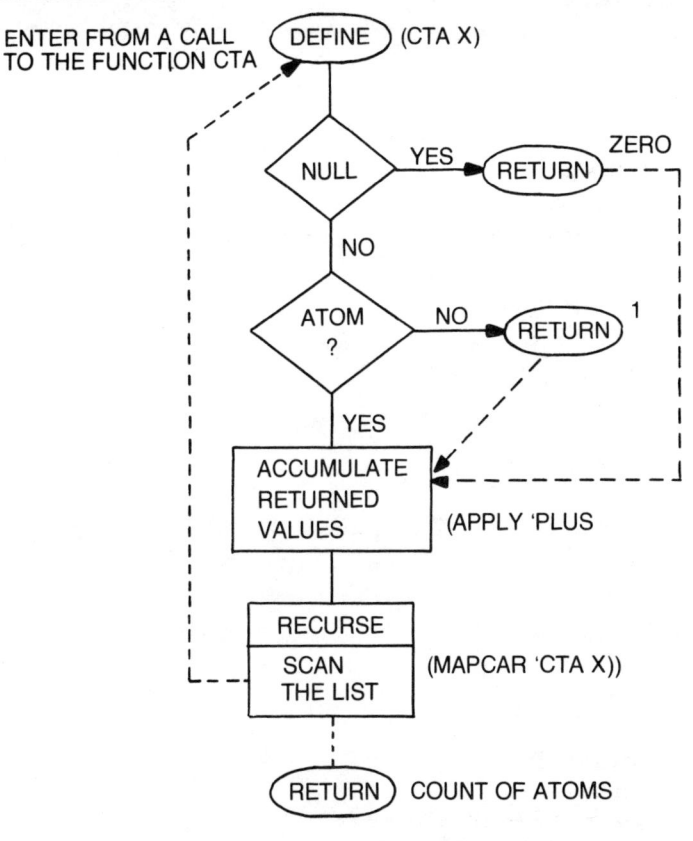

ENTER FROM A CALL TO THE FUNCTION CTA

(DEFINE) (CTA X)

NULL — YES → (RETURN) ZERO

NO

ATOM? — NO → (RETURN) 1

YES

ACCUMULATE RETURNED VALUES (APPLY 'PLUS

RECURSE
SCAN THE LIST (MAPCAR 'CTA X))

(RETURN) COUNT OF ATOMS

NOTE: DASH LINES REFER TO RECURSIVE PATHS.

CSCH (X)

Requirement

To find the CSCH of X.

Program
```
(DEFINE
(CSCH X)
(QUOTIENT 2
(DIFFERENCE
(EXPT 2.718 X)
EXPT 2.718
(MINUS X))))
)
```

Sample Run
```
(SETQ X.1)
(CSCH X)
9.983
********************
(SETQ X .2)
(CSCH X)
4.966
********************
(CSCH 0.3)
3.282
********************
    (CSCH 0.8)
1.125
********************
(CSCH 0.7)
1.318
********************
END
```

Flowchart: CSCH(X)

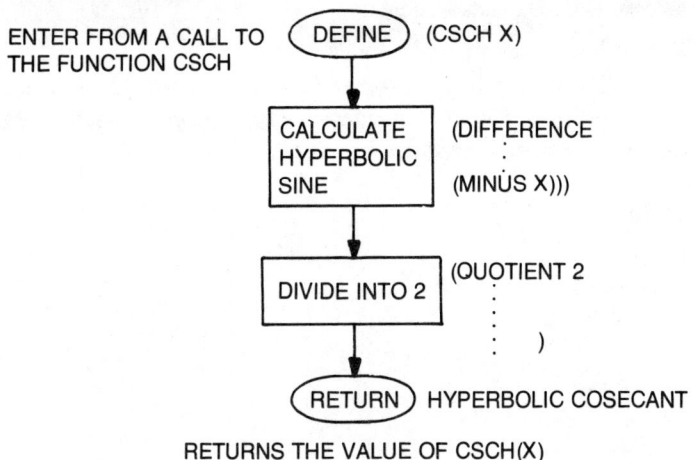

ENTER FROM A CALL TO THE FUNCTION CSCH

(DEFINE) (CSCH X)

CALCULATE HYPERBOLIC SINE — (DIFFERENCE ⋮ (MINUS X)))

DIVIDE INTO 2 — (QUOTIENT 2 ⋮)

(RETURN) HYPERBOLIC COSECANT

RETURNS THE VALUE OF CSCH(X)

DEPTH OF PARENTHESES

Requirement

To find the depth of an S-expression, not counting the first and last parentheses. Depth is the measure of the deepest section of a nested parentheses structure in a list.

Program

```
(DEFINE
(DEPTH L)
((NULL L)
0)
((ATOM (CAR L))
(DEPTH
(CDRL)))
((GREATERP (ADD1
(DEPTH (CAR L)))
(DEPTH(CDR L)))
 (AD1
(DEPTH (CAR L))))
(T
(DEPTH (CDR L)))
))
```

Sample Run

```
(DEPTH '((D) ((A(D)L))))
3
********************
(DEPTH '((((((K))))) J((T))))
5
********************
END
```

DERIVATIVE OF ACOS(X)

Requirement

To find the derivative of ACOS(X).

Program

```
(DEFINE
(DACOS X)
(MINUS
(EXPT
(DIFFERENCE 1
(TIMES X X))
.5))
)
```

Sample Run

```
(DACOS 0.1)
-.99499
********************
(DACOS 0.8)
-.60000
********************
(DACOS 1.0)
-0
********************
(DACOS 0.15)
-.9887
********************
(DACOS 0.6)
-.8000
********************
(DACOS .95)
-.0312
********************
END
```

Flowchart: Derivative of ACOS(X)

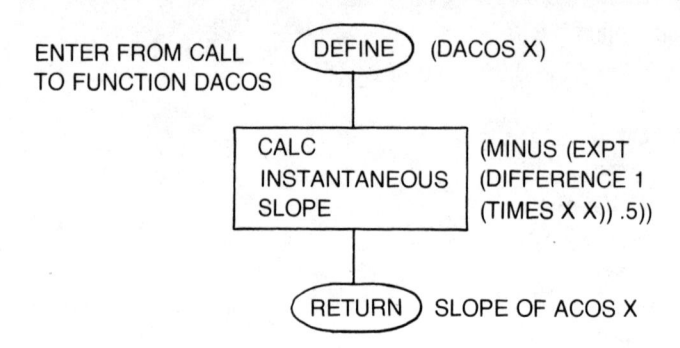

ENTER FROM CALL TO FUNCTION DACOS

(DEFINE) (DACOS X)

| CALC INSTANTANEOUS SLOPE | (MINUS (EXPT (DIFFERENCE 1 (TIMES X X)) .5)) |

(RETURN) SLOPE OF ACOS X

DERIVATIVE OF ACOT(X)

Requirement

To find the ACOT(X) derivative.

Program

```
(DEFINE
(DACOT X)
(MINUS
(QUOTIENT 1
(ADD1
(TIMES X X))))
)
```

Sample Run

```
(SETQ X 0.1)
(DACOT X)
 -.9901
*********************
(SETQ X 0.8)
(DACOT X)
 -.6098
*********************
END
```

Flowchart: Derivative of ACOT(X)

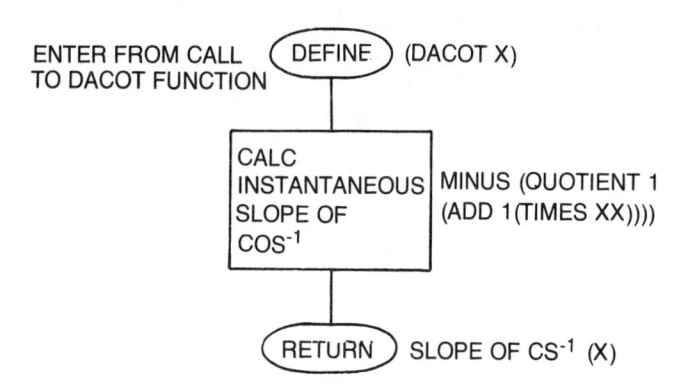

ENTER FROM CALL TO DACOT FUNCTION — (DEFINE) (DACOT X)

CALC INSTANTANEOUS SLOPE OF COS^{-1} | MINUS (QUOTIENT 1 (ADD 1(TIMES XX))))

(RETURN) SLOPE OF CS^{-1} (X)

161

DERIVATIVE OF ASECH(X)

Requirement

To find the derivative of ASECH(X).

Program

```
(DEFINE
(DASECH X)
(MINUS
(RECIP
(TIMES X
EXPT
(DIFFERENCE 1
(TIMES X X))
.5))))
)
```

Sample Run

```
(DASECH .1)
10.05
********************
    (DASECH .4)
2.728
********************
(DASECH .7)
2.000
********************
    (DASECH .6)
2.083
********************
END
```

Flowchart: Derivative of ASECH(X)

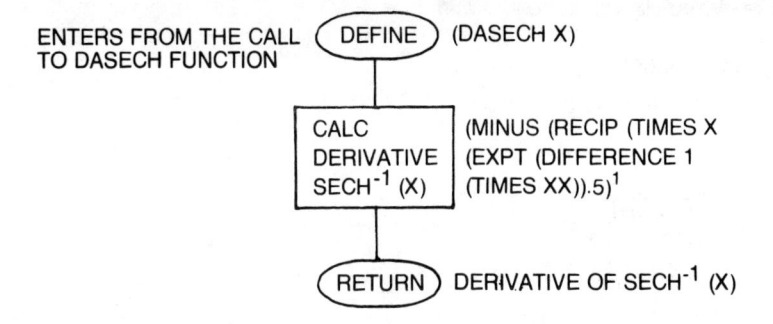

ENTERS FROM THE CALL TO DASECH FUNCTION (DEFINE) (DASECH X)

| CALC DERIVATIVE SECH^{-1} (X) | (MINUS (RECIP (TIMES X (EXPT (DIFFERENCE 1 (TIMES XX)).5)[1] |

(RETURN) DERIVATIVE OF SECH^{-1} (X)

DERIVATIVE OF ATAN (X)

Requirement
To find the derivative of ATAN(X).

Program
```
(DEFINE
(DATAN X)
(QUOTIENT 1)
(ADD1
(TIMES X X)))
)
```

SAMPLE Run
```
(DATAN 0.1)
0.990l
********************
(DATAN 0.8)
0.6098
********************
)DATAN O)
1,000
********************
(DATAN 0.2)
0.9615
*******************
(SETQ X O.5)
(DATAN X)
0.8000
******************

END
```

164

Flowchart: Derivative of ATAN(X)

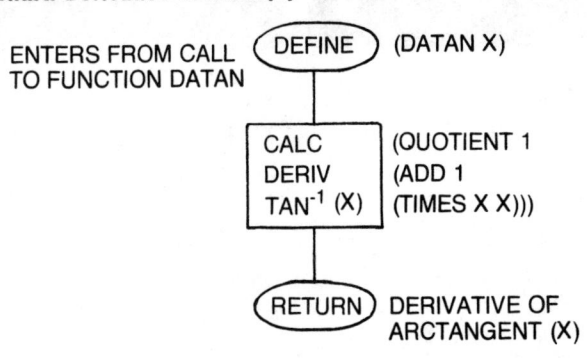

ENTERS FROM CALL TO FUNCTION DATAN — (DEFINE) (DATAN X)

| CALC DERIV TAN^{-1} (X) | (QUOTIENT 1 (ADD 1 (TIMES X X))) |

(RETURN) DERIVATIVE OF ARCTANGENT (X)

DERIVATIVE OF ATANH (X)

Requirement

To find the derivative of ATANH(X)

Program

```
(DEFINE
(DATAH X)
(RECIP
(DIFFERENCE 1
(TIMES X X)))
)
```

Sample Run

```
(DATAH 0.9)
5.263
********************
(DATAH 0.8)
2.778
********************
(DATAH 0.6)
1.563
********************
(DATAH 0.3)
1.099
********************
(DATAH 0.4)
1.190
********************
END
```

Flowchart: Derivative of ATANH(X)

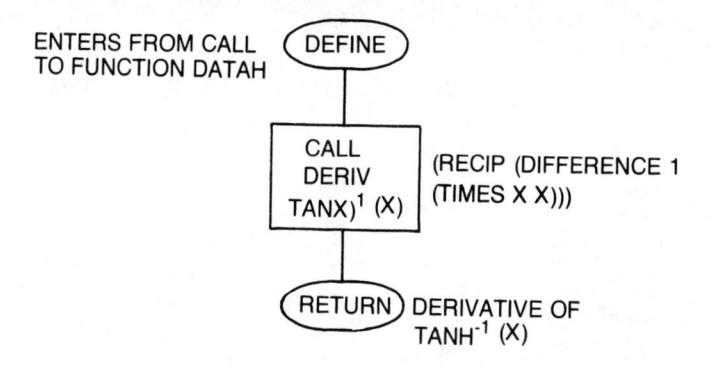

ENTERS FROM CALL TO FUNCTION DATAH → (DEFINE)

CALL DERIV TANX)[1] (X)   (RECIP (DIFFERENCE 1 (TIMES X X)))

(RETURN) DERIVATIVE OF TANH[-1] (X)

DISPLAY THE Nth ATOM

Requirement
To be able to display any Nth atom in a list without altering the list.

Program
```
(DEFINE
(DIS X L)
(COND
((ZEROP
(SUB1 X))
(CAR L))
(T
(DIS (SUB1 X)
(CDR L)))
)))
```

Sample Run
```
(DIS 4 '(HOW ARE YOU TODAY))
TODAY
********************
(DIS 3 '(RED GREEN PINK ORANGE BLUE PURPLE))
PINK
********************
(DIS 5 '(A B C D EF G H I J))
E
********************
(DIS 2 '(MICE ARE NICE))
ARE
********************
(DIS 4 '(THIS IS A TEXT ON LISP))
TEXT
********************
END
```

Flowchart: Display the Nth Atom

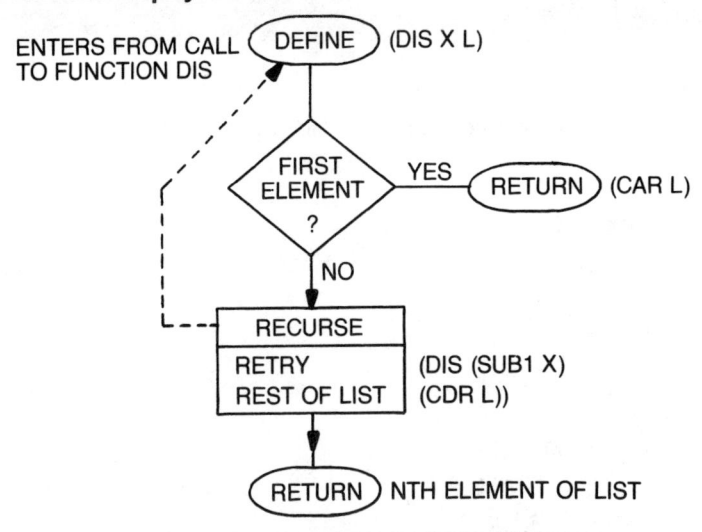

ENTERS FROM CALL TO FUNCTION DIS → **DEFINE** (DIS X L)

↓

FIRST ELEMENT ?
- YES → **RETURN** (CAR L)
- NO ↓

RECURSE
| RETRY | (DIS (SUB1 X) |
| REST OF LIST | (CDR L)) |

↓

RETURN NTH ELEMENT OF LIST

NOTE: DOTTED LINE REFERS TO RECURSION PATHS

169

FACTORIAL

Requirement
A program that generates the factorial of X.

Program
```
(DEFINE
(FACTORIAL X)
(PROG (F)
(SETQ F 1)
AGAIN
(COND
((ZEROP X)
(RETURN F)))
(SETQ F(TIMES F X))
(SETQ X (SUB1 X))
(GO AGAIN)))
```

Sample Run
```
(SETQ X 5)
RUN
120
*******************
(SETQ X 7)
RUN
5040
*******************
(SETQ X 9)
RUN
362880
*******************
(SETQ X 3)
RUN
6
*******************
(SETQ X 8)
RUN
40320
*******************
END
```

FALLING OBJECT

Requirement

To find the time in seconds a solid object will take to fall, where height is either in meters or feet.

Program

```
(DEFINE
(FALL X Y)
(COND
((EQ X'F)
(EXPT
(TIMES 2
(QUOTIENT Y 32.17))
.5))
((EQ X'M)
(EXPT
(TIMES 2
(QUOTIENT Y 9.8))
.5))
))
```

Sample Run

```
(FALL 'F 1)
0.2493
*********************
    (FALL 'M 1)
0.4518
*********************
    (FALL 'F 49)
1.745
*********************
```

END

Flowchart: Falling Object

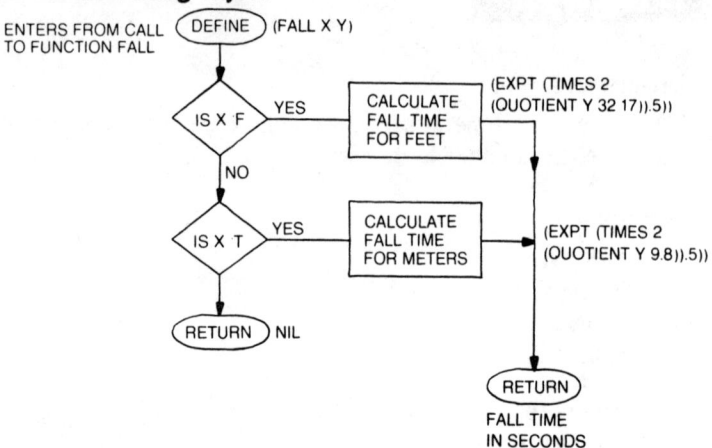

ENTERS FROM CALL TO FUNCTION FALL → DEFINE (FALL X Y)

IS X F — YES → CALCULATE FALL TIME FOR FEET → (EXPT (TIMES 2 (QUOTIENT Y 32 17)).5))

IS X F — NO ↓

IS X T — YES → CALCULATE FALL TIME FOR METERS → (EXPT (TIMES 2 (QUOTIENT Y 9.8)).5))

IS X T — NO ↓

RETURN NIL

RETURN FALL TIME IN SECONDS

FETCH

Requirement
To be able to FETCH information from a DATA-BASE of information contained within the LIST called DATA. The information to be FETCHED is called I. This routine only FETCHES the first occurrence of the element being searched for.

Program
```
(DEFINE
(FET 1)
(PROG (INFO)
(SETQ INFO DATA)
AGAIN
(COND
((NULL INFO)
(RETURN NIL))
((MATCH I (CAR INFO))
(RETURN (CAR INFO))))
(SETQ INFO (CDR INFO))
(GO AGAIN)))
```

Sample Run
Assuming that the DATA-BASE is (LIONS MICE CAT HOUSE DOG).
```
(FET'MICE)
MICE
*********************
(FET'MOOSE)
NIL
*********************
(FET'DOG)
DOG
*********************
```
If the information in the DATA-BASE is in parentheses with more than one ATOM per parentheses you can use the following approach.

Sample Run
Assuming that the data base is ((TREE MOUSE) (TREE HOUSE) (CATS AND DOGS))

```
(FET'(TREE HOUSE))
(TREE HOUSE)
 ********************
(FET & (CATS))
NIL
 ********************
(FET &(CATS))
(CATS AND DOGS)
 ********************
END
```

INDUCTANCE

Requirement
To find the inductance of an inductor.

Program
```
(DEFINE
(IND X FREQ)
(QUOTIENT X
(TIMES 2
(TIMES FREQ
3.14159)))
)
```

Sample Run
```
(SETQ X 1)
(SETQ FREQ 1000)
(IND X FREQ)
0.000159
********************
(SETQ X 2)
(SETQ FREQ 2000)
(IND X FREQ)
0.000159
********************
(IND 3 2000)
0.000318
********************
(IND 5 2000)
0.000397
********************
    END
```

Flowchart: Inductance

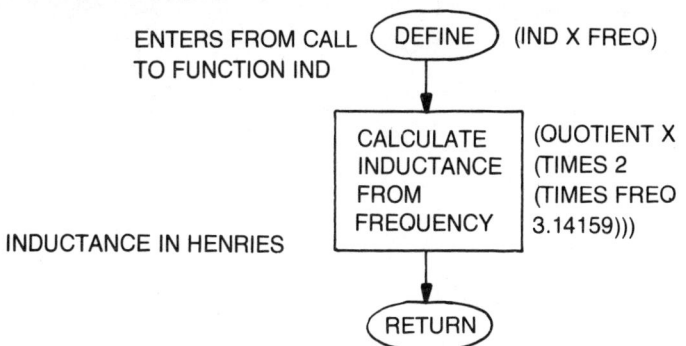

ENTERS FROM CALL TO FUNCTION IND — (DEFINE) (IND X FREQ)

CALCULATE INDUCTANCE FROM FREQUENCY — (QUOTIENT X (TIMES 2 (TIMES FREQ 3.14159)))

INDUCTANCE IN HENRIES

(RETURN)

175

IMAGINARY PART OF A COMPLEX NUMBER

Requirement
To find the value of the imaginary part of a complex variable.

Program
```
(DEFINE
(IPC A)
(CAR
(CDR A))
)
```

SAMPLE RUN

```
(SETQ A '(1 0))
(IPC A)
0
*********************
(SETQ A '(2 1))
(IPC A)
1
*********************
(IPC '(3 2))
2
*********************
(IPC '(4 3))
3
*********************
    (IPC 6(7 9))
9
*********************
END
```

Flowchart: Imaginary Part of a Complex Number

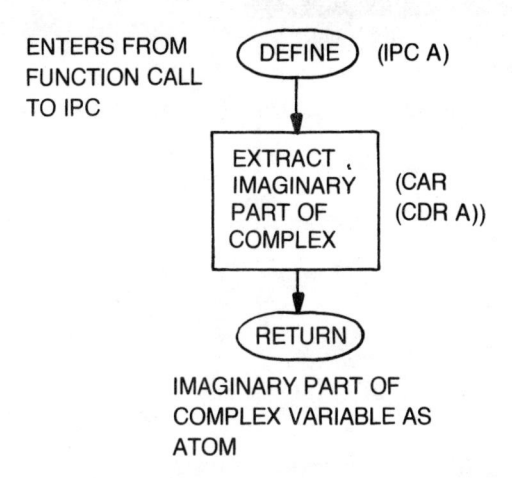

ENTERS FROM FUNCTION CALL TO IPC

(DEFINE) (IPC A)

EXTRACT IMAGINARY PART OF COMPLEX   (CAR (CDR A))

(RETURN)

IMAGINARY PART OF COMPLEX VARIABLE AS ATOM

INSERTION OF AN ATOM NO. 1

Requirement

To be able to insert an ATOM to the right of the named ATOM in a LIST.

Program

```
(DEFINE
(INSTR AO AN L)
(COND
((NULL L)
( ))
((EQ (CAR L)
AO)
(CONS AO
(CONS AN
(CDR L))))
(T
(CONS (CAR L)
INSTR AO AN (CDR L))))
)))
```

Sample Run

```
(SETQ L '(MICE NICE))
(SETQ AO 'MICE)
(SETQ AN 'ARE)
(INSTR AO AN L)
(MICE ARE NICE)
********************
(SETQ L '(THE DEVIL HERE)
(SETQ AO 'DEVIL)
(SETQ AN 'IS)
(INSTR AO AN L)
(THE DEVIL IS HERE)
********************
    END
```

INSERTION OF AN ATOM NO. 2

Requirement
To be able to insert a given ATOM to the left of the named ATOM in a list.

Program
```
(DEFINE
(INSTL OA NA L)
(COND
((NULL L
( ))
((EQ (CAR L)
OA)
(CONS NA
(CONS (CAR L)
(CDR L))))
(T
(CONS (CAR L)
(INSTL OA NA (CDR L))))
)))
```

Sample Run
```
(SETQ OA 'ARE)
(SETQ NA 'MICE)
(SETQ L '(ARE NICE)
(INSTL OA NA L)
(MICE ARE NICE)
********************
(INSTL 'IS 'THIS '(IS LISP))
(THIS IS
********************
END
```

JOULE'S LAW

Requirement

To find the number of calories produced by a given current through a given resistance over a given time.

Program

```
(DEFINE
(CAL I T R)
(QUOTIENT
(TIMES I
(TIMES I
(TIMES R T)))
4.19)
)
```

Sample Run

```
(SETQ I 1)
(SETQ T 2)
(SETQ R 3)
(CAL I T R)
1.432
```
****
```
    (CAL 4 5 6)
114.558
```
****
```
(CAL 7 8 9
842. 005
```
****
```
    END
```

Flowchart: Joule's Law

ENTERS FROM THE FUNCTION CALL TO CAL → (DEFINE) (CAL I T R)

↓

| CALCULATE HEAT FROM CURRENT, RESISTANCE, TIME | (QUOTIENT (TIMES I (TIMES I (TIMES R T))) 4.19) |

↓

(RETURN)

HEAT IN CALORIES

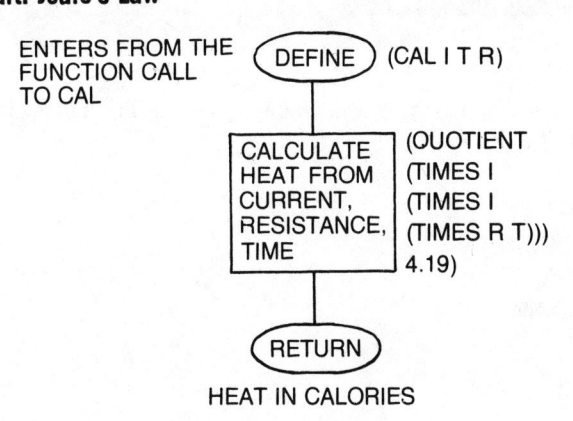

LIST OF FIRST ATOMS

Requirementl

To produce a list that contains the first ATOM of each of the SUB-LISTS in the LIST.

Program

```
(DEFINE
(FAL L)
(COND
((NULL)
( ))
(T
(CONS (CAR (CAR L))
(FAL (CDR L))))
))
```

Sample Run

```
(FAL'((T R)(Y U)(I.))
(T Y I)
********************
(FAL'((MICE ARE)(NICE TO)(EAT WITH)(RICE SOME-
TIMES))
(MICE NICE EAT RICE)
********************
(SETQ L '((F G)(J K)(E R))
(FAL L)
(F J E)
********************
(SETQ L '((VGF TRD(BHU KRF)(NKU DFT))
(FAL L)
(VGF BHU

********************
END
```

MAPPING (ONE TO ONE)

Requirement

To search one list which contains numeric quantities and find the largest value and then select from a second list the item which is in the same relative position as the first one picked.

Program
```
     DEFINE((
     (SEL (LAMBDA (L M)
     (PROG(A B U V Y Z)
     (SETQ A (CAR L))
     (SETQ B(CAR M))
     (SETQ U (CDR L))
     (SETQ V (CDR M))
         AGAIN
     (COND
     ((NULL U)
     (RETURN B)))
     (SETQ Y (CAR U))
     (SETQ Z (CAR V))
     (SETQ U (CDR U))
     (SETQV (CDR V))
     (COND
     ((GREATER Y A)
     (PROG2 (SETQ A Y)
     (SETQ B Z))))
     (GO AGAIN)
     )))))
```

Sample Run
```
     (SETQ L'(1 8 56 7))
     (SETQ M'(M I C E))
     RUN
     C
*********************
     End
```

MATCHING

Requirement
To define a function that allows matching of two lists.

Program
```
    (DEFINE
(MATCH X Y)
(COND((AND (NULL X)(NULL Y))
T)
((OR (NULL X)(NULL Y))
NIL)
    ((OR (EQUAL (CAR X) '?)
    (EQUAL (CAR X)(CAR Y)))
    (MATCH (CDR X)(CDR Y))
    ((EQUAL (CAR X) '
    (COND
    ((MATCH (CDR X)
    Y))
    ((MATCH (CDR X) (CDR Y)))
    ((MATCH X (CDR Y)) )))))
```

This matching routine allows the use of special ATOMS? and *, ? is used to replace a single ATOM in the comparison, while allows you to replace more than one ATOM. When using the MATCH function, the order must be written (MATCH A B) in order to match.

Sample Run
```
    (MATCH '(MICE ARE NICE) '(MICE ARE NICE))
    T
    ********************
    (MATCH '(ARE '(MICE ARE NICE))
    T
    ********************
    (MATCH '(MICE ARE?)'(MICE ARE NICE))
    T
    END.
```

VECTOR VALUE

Requirement
To find the maximum value in a vector.

Program
```
(DEFINE
(MV L)
( OND
((NULL (CDR L))
(CAR L))
((GREATERP (CAR L)
(CAR (CDR L)))
(MV
(CONS (CAR L)
(CDR (CDR L)))))
(T
(MV (CDR L)))
))
```

Sample Run
```
(MV '(4 8 6 9 3))
9
********************
(MV '(78 654 890 567))
890
********************
(MV '(11 111 8 1111))
1111
********************
END
```

PARALLEL RESISTANCE

Requirement

To find the total parallel resistance of any two resistances).

Program

```
(DEFINE
(PR R1 R2)
(QUOTIENT
(TIMES R1 R2)
(PLUS R1 R2))
)
```

Sample Run

```
(SETQ R1 1)
   (SETQ R2 1)
(PR R1 R2)
0.5000
   ********************
(PR 1 2)
0.6000
   ********************
(PR 1 3)
0.750
   ********************
   (PR 2 8)
1.6000
   ********************
END
```

Flowchart: Parallel Resistance

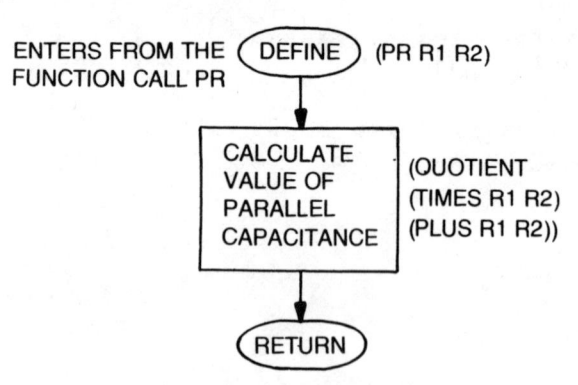

ENTERS FROM THE FUNCTION CALL PR → (DEFINE) (PR R1 R2)

CALCULATE VALUE OF PARALLEL CAPACITANCE — (QUOTIENT (TIMES R1 R2) (PLUS R1 R2))

RETURN

PARALLEL RESISTANCE IN OHMS

186

PERCENTAGE CHANGE

Requirement

To find the percentage change from Y to X.

Program

```
(DEFINE
 (PC X Y)
 (QUOTIENT
  (TIMES
   (DIFFERENCE X Y)
   100)
  Y)
)
```

Sample Run

```
(PC 1 1)
0
********************
(PC 2 1)
100.00
********************
(PC 3 1)
200.00
********************
(PC 4 1)
300.00
********************
(PC 5 2)
150.00
********************
END
```

Flowchart: Percentage Change

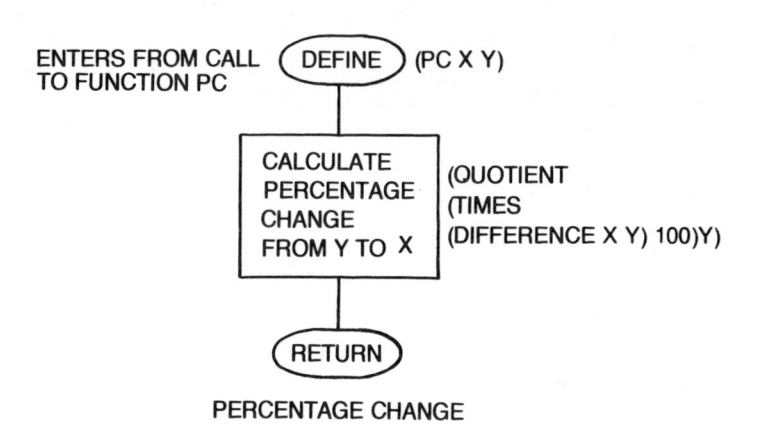

ENTERS FROM CALL TO FUNCTION PC → (DEFINE) (PC X Y)

CALCULATE PERCENTAGE CHANGE FROM Y TO X — (QUOTIENT (TIMES (DIFFERENCE X Y) 100)Y)

(RETURN)

PERCENTAGE CHANGE

POWER (ANY POSITIVE INTEGER)

Requirement
X to the Y power where Y is any positive integer. This is a recursive power function.

Program
```
(DEFINE (PWR X Y)
(COND ((ZEROP Y)
1)
((TIMES X
(PWR X
(SUB1 Y))))))
   X
    (SUB1 Y))))))
```

Sample Run
```
(PWR 4 5)
256
**********
(PWR 6.90)
1
**********
(PWR 54 1)
54
**********
(PWR 3 8)
6561
**********
(PWR 10 4)
1000
**********
(PWR 5.53)
166.375
**********
(PWR 4 4)
256
**********
END
```

Flowchart: Power (Any Positive Integer)

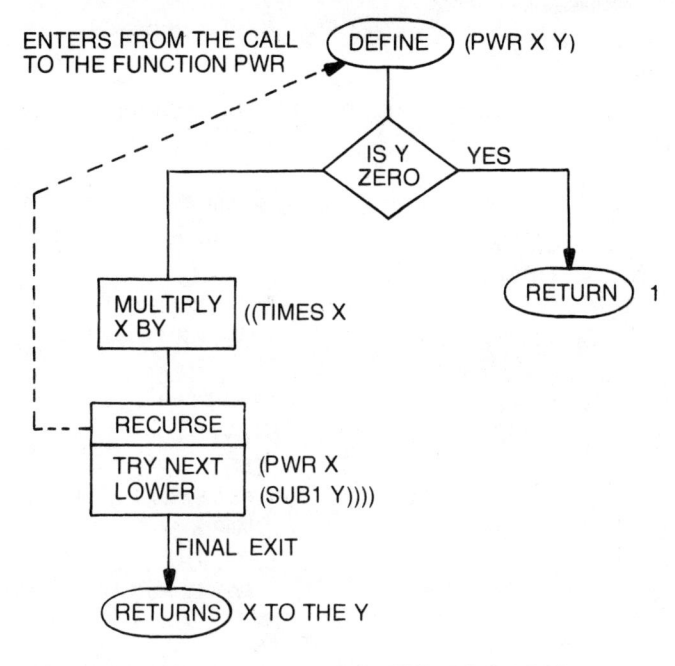

ENTERS FROM THE CALL TO THE FUNCTION PWR → (DEFINE) (PWR X Y)

IS Y ZERO — YES → (RETURN) 1

MULTIPLY X BY ((TIMES X

RECURSE
TRY NEXT LOWER (PWR X (SUB1 Y))))

FINAL EXIT
(RETURNS) X TO THE Y

NOTE: THE DASHED LINE IS THE RECURSION PATH

POWER (PRIMITIVE)

Requirement

X to the Y power where Y is 0, 1 or 2. This is a primitive power function.

Program

```
(DEFINE(PWR X Y)
(COND ((EQUAL Y O)
1)
((EQUAL Y 1)
X)
((EQUAL Y 2)
(TIMES X X))))
```

Sample Run

```
(PWR 5 0)
1
***********
(PWR 67 1)
67
**********
(PWR 34 2)
1156
**********
(PWR 4.16 2)
17.3056
**********
(PWR 567 1)
567
**********
(PWR 34.9 0)
1
**********
END
```

Flowchart: Power (Primitive)

ENTERS FROM CALL TO FUNCTION PWR → (DEFINE) (PWR X Y)

$y = 0$? — YES → (RETURN) O

NO ↓

$y = 1$? — YES → (RETURN) X

NO → (TIMES X X) (RETURN) X^2

PSYCHIATRIST

Requirement
This program is designed to simulate a psychiatrist. It is quite elementary, yet it can respond with a dialogue for at least a few steps. This program is only a demonstration. It builds no model of the problem since it depends on keywords supplied by the user.

Program
```
(DEFINE (PSY)
(PROG (K FRIEND U)
(PRINT ' (I AM WAITING!))
AGAIN
(SETQ U (READ))
(COND ((MATCH
'(I AM SCARED (U)
(PRINT(APEND
'(HOW LONG HAVE YOU BEEN SCARED)
K)))
((MATCH
'( FRIEND ) U)
(SETQ FRIEND T)
(PRINT '(TELL ME MORE ABOUT YOUR FRIENDS)))
((MATCH '(COMPUTERS ) U)
(PRINT '(DO COMPUTERS SCARE YOU)))
(( OR (MATCH '(NO) &) (MATCH '(YES) U))
(PRINT '(PLEASE DO NOT BE FRIGHTEN)))
((MATCH '( (RESTRICT ? BADWORD) ) U)
(PRINT '(PLEASE USE OTHER PHRASES)))
(FRIEND (SETQ FRIEND NIL)
(PRINT '(BEFORE YOU SPOKE OF YOUR FRIEND)))
(T(PRINT '(I AM SORRY I MUST GO NOW))
(RETURN 'BYE))) (GO AGAIN)))
```

Sample Run
(I AM WAITING)
(I AM SCARED ABOUT A FRIEND)
(HOW LONG HAVE YOU BEEN SCARED ABOUT A FRIEND)
(ALWAYS AFTER TALKING TO MY FRIEND)

(TELL ME MORE ABOUT YOUR FRIEND)
(THEY ALL PROGRAM COMPUTERS)
(DO COMPUTERS SCARE YOU)
(YES)
(PLEASE DO NOT BE FRIGHTEN)
(I WILL TRY NOT TO BE)
(BEFORE YOU SPOKE OF YOUR FRIEND)

This is one program that is fun to play with by changing the "keywords" in the program or expanding it.

REAL PART OF A COMPLEX NUMBER

Requirement
To find the real part of the complex number given or to secure the first element in a list.

Program
(DEFINE
(RPC A)
(CAR

Sample Run
(RPC '(4 5))
4
****
(RPC '(56 78))
56
****
(RPC '(-8 -90))
-8
****
(RPC '(2 67))
2
(RPC '(APPLE ORANGE))
APPLE
****
(RPC '(A 56))
A
****
END

REAL TO COMPLEX CONVERSION

Requirement

To take two real numbers and transpose them to complex notation. Also useful in placing two elements into a list.

Program

```
(DEFINE
(RCC A B)
(CONS A
(CONS B NIL))
)
```

Sample Run

```
(RCC 1 0)
(1 0)
********************
(SETQ A 2)
(SETQ B 3)
(RCC A B)
(2 3)
********************
(SETQ A 4)
(SETQ B 5)
(RCC A B)
(4 5)
********************
(RCC 6 7)
(6 7)
********************
END
```

Flowchart: Real to Complex Conversion

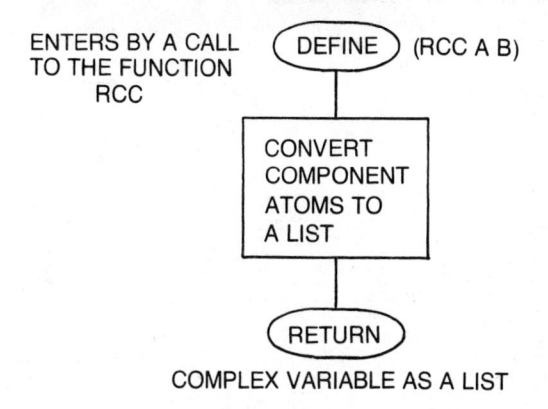

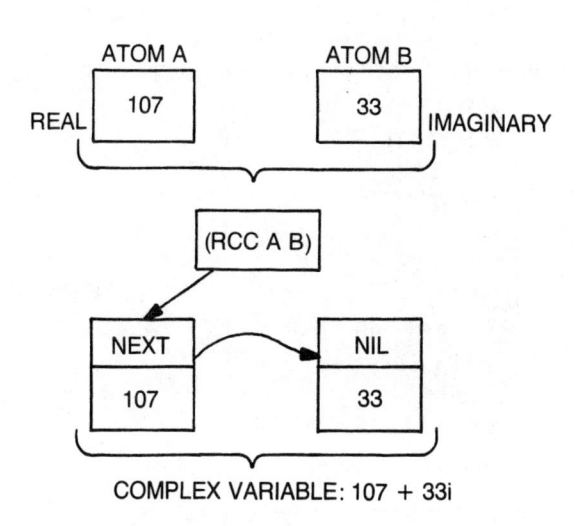

ENTERS BY A CALL TO THE FUNCTION RCC

DEFINE (RCC A B)

CONVERT COMPONENT ATOMS TO A LIST

RETURN

COMPLEX VARIABLE AS A LIST

ATOM A: 107 (REAL)
ATOM B: 33 (IMAGINARY)

(RCC A B)

NEXT — 107 → NIL — 33

COMPLEX VARIABLE: 107 + 33i

RECTANGULAR POLAR MOMENT

Requirement
To find the polar moment of inertia of a rectangle.

Program
```
(DEFINE
(RPM B H)
(QUOTIENT
(TIMES B
(TIMES H
(PLUS
(TIMES B B)
(TIMES H H))))
12)
)
```

Sample Run
```
(SETQ B 1)
(SETQ H 1)
(RPM B H)
0.16667
********************
(RPM 1 2)
0.83333
********************
(RPM 1 3)
2.5000
********************
END
```

Flowchart: Rectangular Polar Moment

FLOWCHART: RECTANGULAR POLAR MOMENT

ENTERS BY THE FUNCTION CALL RPM — (DEFINE) (RPM B H)

CALCULATE POLAR MOMENT — (QUOTIENT (TIMES B (TIMES H (PLUS (TIMES B B) (TIMES H H)))) 12)

(RETURN)
POLAR MOMENT OF INERTIA

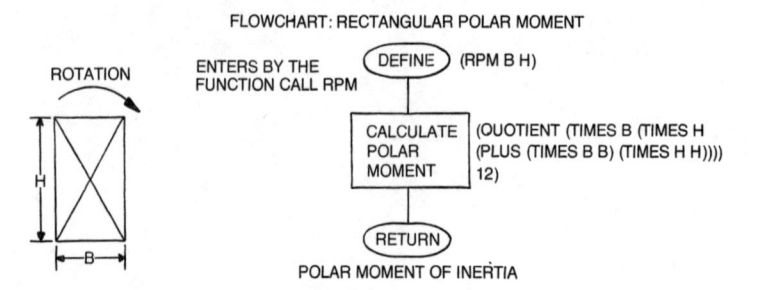

REMOVE

Requirement
To be able to use a list as a data-base and remove information from this data base. Data is the name of the data base and I is the information to be removed. If the information I was indeed in the data base it will be printed, if not, then no result.

Program
```
(DEFINE
(REM I)
(COND ((MEMBER
I DATA)
(SETQ DATA
(DELETE I I)))
```

Sample Run
Assume that the data base contains MOUSE LION CAT
(REM I) where I is LION
LION
****
(REM I) where I is MICE
****
(REM I) where I is CAT
CAT
****
END

REMOVE AN ATOM FROM A LIST

Requirement
To be able to remove an ATOM from a list at its first occurrence

Program
```
(DEFINE
(REM A L)
(COND
((NULL L) ( ))
((EQ (CAR L) A)
(CDR L))
(T
(CONS (CAR L)
(REM A (CDR L))))
))
```

Sample Run
```
(REM 'ARE '(MICE ARE NICE))
(MICE NICE)
********************
(REM'S '(T R S U))
(T R U)

********************

(REM 'GIRLS '(BOYS LIKE GIRLS))
(BOYS LIKE)
********************
(REM 'I '(I LIKE BANANAS))
(LIKE BANANAS)
********************
(SETQ A 'KEN)
(SETQ L '(KEN IS AN AUTHOR))
(REM A L)
(IS AN AUTHOR)
********************
END
```

REMOVE THE NUMBERS

Requirement
To remove selectively only the elements from a list which are numbers but leave the rest of the ATOMS.

Program
```
(DEFINE
(RAN L)
(COND
((NULL L
( ))
((NUMBERP (CAR L))
(RAN (CDR L)))
(T
(CONS (CAR L)
(RAN (CDR L))))
))
```

Sample Run
```
(RAN '(6 BEARS 7 MICE 9 MONKEYS))
(BEARS MICE MONKEYS)
********************
(RAN '(3 MICE ARE 2 TIMES BETTER THAN 4 RICE))
(MICE ARE TIMES BETTER THAN RICE)
********************
(RAN '(THERE ARE 44 DEAD STONE LIONS))
(THERE ARE DEAD STONE LIONS)
********************
END
```

REPLACEMENT

Requirement
To replace the first occurrence of an atom in a list with another atom.

Program
```
(DEFINE
(SUB OA NA L)
(COND
((NULL L
( ))
((EQ (CAR L)
OA)
(CONS NA (CDR L)))
(T
(CONS (CAR L)
(SUB OA NA (CDR L))))
)))
```

Sample Run
```
(SETQ OA 'ARE)
(SETQ NA 'AREN'T)
(SETQ L '(MICE ARE NICE))
(SUB OA NA L)
(MICR AREN'T NICE)
********************
(SUB 'BEANS ' BANANAS ' '( BEANS ARE FRUIT))
BANANAS ARE FRUIT)
********************
END
```

REVERSE

Requirement

To be able to reverse the order of the ATOMS in a list.

Program
```
DEFINE((
(RE(LAMBDA (K) (PROG (J N)
(SETQ J K)
(SETQ N NIL)
AGAIN
(COND
((NULL J)
(RETURN N)))
(SETQ N(CONS (CAR J) N))
(SETQ J (CDR J))
GO AGAIN)
)))))
```

Sample Run
```
(SETQ X'(A B C D))
RUN
(D C B A)
*********************
(SETQ X '(1 6 8 4 8))
RUN
(8 4 8 6 1)
*********************
(SETQ X '(M I C E))
RUN
(E C I M)
*********************
(SETQ X '(L I S P))
RUN
(P S I L)
*********************
END
```

SECH (X)

Requirement

To find SECH(X).

Program

```
(DEFINE
(SECH X)
RECIP
(QUOTIENT
(PLUS
(EXPT 2.718 X)
RECIP
(EXPT 2.718 X)))
2))
)
```

Sample Run

```
(SECH .1)
0.9950
*********************
(SECH .2)
.9803)
*********************
(SECH .5)
.8868
*********************
(SETQ X .6)
(SECH X)
.8435
*********************
END
```

Flowchart: SECH(X)

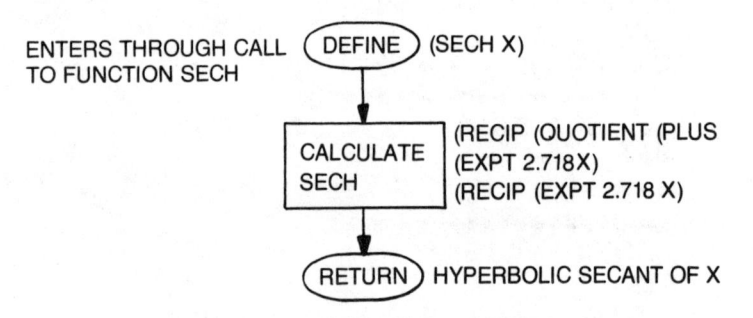

ENTERS THROUGH CALL TO FUNCTION SECH → (DEFINE) (SECH X)

CALCULATE SECH: (RECIP (QUOTIENT (PLUS (EXPT 2.718 X) (RECIP (EXPT 2.718 X))

(RETURN) HYPERBOLIC SECANT OF X

NOTE: THE ATOM 2.718 REPRESENTS THE MATHEMATICAL CONSTANT e.

SINH (X)

Requirement
To find the value of SINH (X).

Program
```
(DEFINE
(SINH X)
(QUOTIENT
(DIFFERENCE
(EXPT 2,718 X)
(EXPT 2.718
(MINUS X)))
2)
)
```

Sample Run
```
(SETQ X 1)
(SINH X)
1.175
 **********
(SETQ X 2)
(SINH X)
3.627
 **********
(SETQ X 3)
(SINH X)
10.02
 **********
END
```

Flowchart: SINH(X)

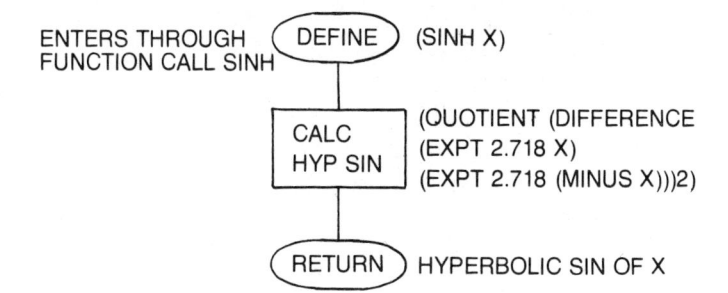

ENTERS THROUGH FUNCTION CALL SINH — (DEFINE) (SINH X)

CALC HYP SIN — (QUOTIENT (DIFFERENCE (EXPT 2.718 X) (EXPT 2.718 (MINUS X)))2)

(RETURN) HYPERBOLIC SIN OF X

203

TANH (X)

Requirement
To find the value of TANH (X).

Program
```
(DEFINE
(TANH X)
(QUOTIENT
(DIFFERENCE
(EXPT 2.718 X)
RECIP
(EXPT 2.718 X)))
(MINUS X))))
)
```

Sample Run
```
(TANH 2)
.9640
**********
(TANH 1)
.7616
*********
(TANH 4)
.9993
**********
END
```

Flowchart: TANH(X)

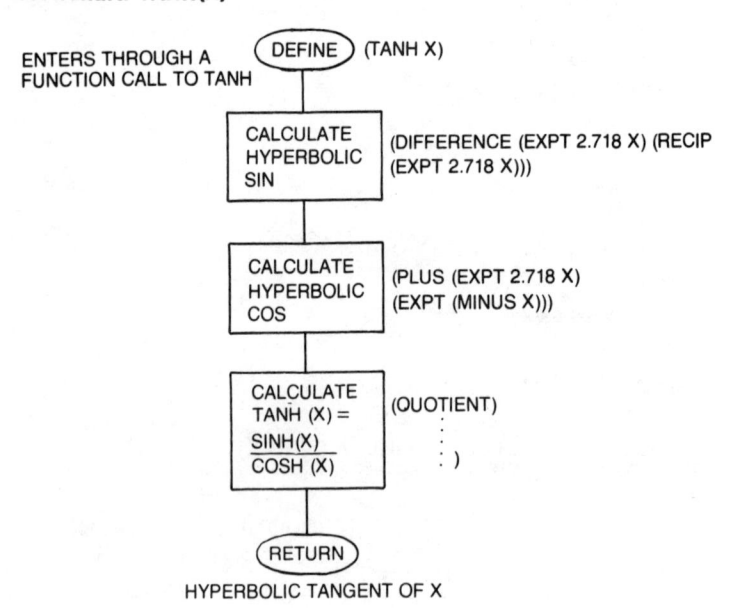

ENTERS THROUGH A FUNCTION CALL TO TANH

(DEFINE) (TANH X)

CALCULATE HYPERBOLIC SIN — (DIFFERENCE (EXPT 2.718 X) (RECIP (EXPT 2.718 X)))

CALCULATE HYPERBOLIC COS — (PLUS (EXPT 2.718 X) (EXPT (MINUS X)))

CALCULATE TANH (X) = $\frac{SINH(X)}{COSH(X)}$ — (QUOTIENT ⋮)

(RETURN)

HYPERBOLIC TANGENT OF X

VECTOR ADDITION

Requirement
To be able to add any two vectors.

Program
```
(DEFINE
(VADD V1 V2)
(COND
((NULL V2)
V2)
((NULL V2)
V1)
(T
(CONS
(PLUS (CAR V1)
(CAR V2)
(VADD (CDR V1)(CDR V2))))
)))
```

Sample Run
```
(SETQ V1 '(1 2 3 4))
(SETQ V2 '(5 6 7 8))
(VADD V1 V2)
(6 8 10 12)
********************
(VADD '(6 7 8) '(3 3 3))
(9 10 11)
********************
(VAD '(2 2 2 2) '(4 5 6 7))
(6 7 8 9)
********************
```
END

VECTOR CROSS PRODUCT

Requirement

To find the vector cross product between two vectors.

Program

```
(DEFINE
(VCP A B)
(SETQ X 1)
(CAR A))
(SETQ X2)
(CAR B))
(SETQ Y1)
(CAR (CDR A)))
(SETQ Y2)
(CAR ( DR B)))
(SETQ Z1)
(CAR (CDR (CDR A))))
(SETQ Z2)
(CAR(CDR(CDR B))))
(SETQ X3
(DIFFERENCE
(TIMES Y1 Z2)
(TIMES Z1 Y2)))
(SETQ Y3
(DIFFERENCE
(TIMES Z1 X2)
(TIMES X1 Z2)))
(SETQ Z3
(DIFFERENCE
(TIMES X1 Y2)
(TIMES X2 Y1)))
 CONS X3
(CONS Y3
(CONS Z3 NIL)))
.)
```

Sample Run

```
(VCP '(1 2 3) '(4 5 6))
(-3 6 -3)
```
****

```
(VCP '(7 8 9) '(10 11 12))
(-3 6 -3)
*********************
(VCP '(1 2 3) '(7 8 9))
(-6 12 -6)
*********************
(VCP '(1 2 3) '(12 11 10))
(-13 26 -13)
*********************
(VCP '(3 1 2) '(4 5 6))
(-4 -10 11)
*********************
END
```

Flowchart: Vector Cross Product

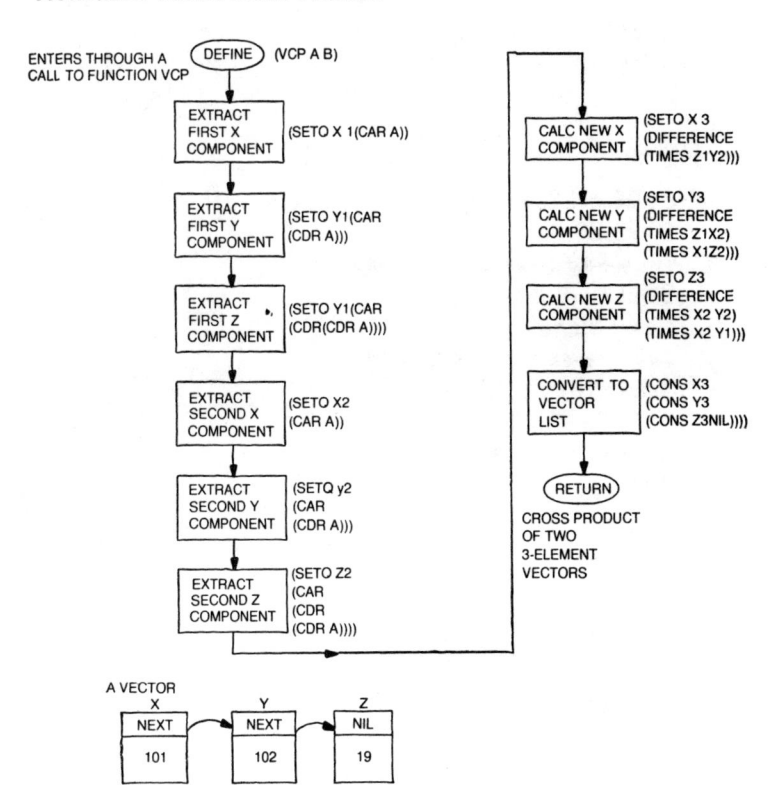

ENTERS THROUGH A CALL TO FUNCTION VCP

(DEFINE) (VCP A B)

EXTRACT FIRST X COMPONENT	(SETO X 1(CAR A))
EXTRACT FIRST Y COMPONENT	(SETO Y1(CAR (CDR A)))
EXTRACT FIRST Z COMPONENT	(SETO Y1(CAR (CDR(CDR A))))
EXTRACT SECOND X COMPONENT	(SETO X2 (CAR A))
EXTRACT SECOND Y COMPONENT	(SETQ y2 (CAR (CDR A)))
EXTRACT SECOND Z COMPONENT	(SETO Z2 (CAR (CDR (CDR A))))
CALC NEW X COMPONENT	(SETO X 3 (DIFFERENCE (TIMES Z1Y2)))
CALC NEW Y COMPONENT	(SETO Y3 (DIFFERENCE (TIMES Z1X2) (TIMES X1Z2)))
CALC NEW Z COMPONENT	(SETO Z3 (DIFFERENCE (TIMES X2 Y2) (TIMES X2 Y1)))
CONVERT TO VECTOR LIST	(CONS X3 (CONS Y3 (CONS Z3NIL))))

(RETURN)

CROSS PRODUCT OF TWO 3-ELEMENT VECTORS

A VECTOR

X	Y	Z
NEXT	NEXT	NIL
101	102	19

207

VECTOR MULTIPLIED BY A SCALAR

Requirement

To multiply a vector by a scalar and create a new vector.

Program

```
(DEFINE
(SVEC X L)
(COND
((NULL L)
( ))
(T
(CONS
(TIMES X
(CAR L))
(SVEC X
(CDR L))))
))
```

Sample Run

```
(SVEC 5 '(3 5 6 7))
(15 25 30 35)
********************
(SVEC 8'(6 5 4 6))
(48 40 32 48)
********************
(SVEC 10 '(21 17 13 4))
(210 170 130 40)
********************
END
```

VECTOR TEST FOR ALL ZEROS

Requirement
Checks a vector to determine whether or not it is all zeros.

Program
```
(DEFINE
(ZVT L)
(COND
((NULL L)
( ) )
T)
((ZEROP
(CAR L))
(ZVT
(CDR L)))
(T NIL)
))
```

Sample Run
```
(ZVT '(0 0 9 0))
NIL
********************
(ZVT '( 0 0 0 0 0 0 0))
T
********************
(ZVT '(8 0 7 0 6))
NIL

(ZVT '(0 0))
T

END
```

Index

A
ACOT derivative of	159-161
Add	122 123
Addition complex	134 135
Algebraic functions	10-13
Annular moment of inertia	124 125
Annular polar moment	126. 127
Artificial intelligence	115-120
ASECH. derivative of	162. 163
ATAMH. derivative of	166. 167
ATAN. derivative of	164. 165
Atom check	128 129
Atom member of a list	130 131
Atom No 1. insertion	178
Atom No 2 insertion	179
Atom. remove from a list	198
Atoms	16-18
list of first	182

C
Circular polar moment	132 133
Common LISP functions	39-60
Conjugate. complex	136. 137
Complex conversion real	194 195
Complex number	
imaginary part	176 177
real part	193
COSH	150 151
COTH	152 153
Count	154 155
CSCH	156 157

D
Depth of parentheses	158
Division. complex	138 139
Dot notation	86 87

E
Expressions	13-16

F
Factorial	170
Falling object	171 172
Fetch	173
First review	34 35
Functions in LISP	35-39

G
General list	87-89

I
Imaginary part	
of a complex number	176 177
Inductance	175
Input output	106-108

J
Joule's Law	180 181

L
LISP	112 115
common functions	39-60
functions	35-39
parameters	63-65
system	29-31
List processing	65-71

Lists	21-25
Logic	61-63

M
Mapping	183
Matching	184
Multiplication. complex	140. 141

N
Nth Atom. display of	168. 169
Numbers, remove	199

P
Parallel resistance	186
Percentage change	187
Predicates	71-74
how they're used	76-78
Power (any positive integer)	188. 189
(primitive)	190
Programming	93-106
more on	95
Psychiatrist	191

R
Reciprocal. complex	142. 143
Rectangular polar moment	196
Recursion	27-29
two list	89-92
Recursive functions	78-81
Recursive list processing	81-86
Remove	197
Remove an atom	
from a list	198
Replacement	200
Reverse	201
Review	92. 93. 108-112
first	34. 35
second	74-76

S
SECH	202
Second review	74-76
SINH	203
Square. complex	146. 147
Square root.	
complex	148. 149
Subexpressions	32-34
Sublists	25. 26
Subtraction complex	144. 145
Symbols	18-21

T
TANH	204
Two list recursion	89-92

V
Vector addition	205
Vector cross product	206. 207
Vector multiplied by a scalar	208
Vector test for all zeros	209
Vector value	185

Z
Zeros vector test	209